Rory Ridley-Duff

The Case for FairShares

A new model for social enterprise development
and the strengthening of the
social and solidarity economy

by

Rory Ridley-Duff

The FairShares Model is a project of
Social Enterprise Europe Ltd

The Case for FairShares

Copyright © 2015, Rory Ridley-Duff

Except where stated otherwise, this book and its content is licensed for use by the general public under a BY-NC-ND Creative Commons 4.0 International Licence.

Except where stated otherwise, the content of this book is licensed for use by members and supporters of the FairShares Association under a BY-SA Creative Commons 4.0 International Licence. A supporter is a person who has taken out an annual subscription to the FairShares Association or who has registered their interest by joining the FairShares Online Community on Loomio. A member is a person listed in the Founder, Labour or User Members sub-group of the FairShares Online Community.

Creative Commons Acknowledgements

The following people have generously contributed to the development of FairShares IP included in this document. It is reproduced under Creative Commons licensing and the author acknowledges their contribution to this work. Please credit them as well as the author of this book if you reproduce their figures, diagrams, social auditing or advanced diagnostic tools.

Mike Bull

- The Rise of Solidarity Co-operatives, Part 1, (co-authored)
- Understanding Social Enterprise activities (co-authored)
- Figure 1.1 – Historical influences on FairShares
- Figure 1.2 – FairShares as a solidarity cooperative
- Activity 2.4 – Level 1 governance audit
- Activity 2.7 – Advanced governance diagnostics

Tracey Coule

- Activity 2.4 – Level 1 governance audit
- Activity 2.7 – Advanced governance diagnostics

Nicola Dickins

- Activity 2.2 – Level 1 social audit
- The FairShares Model (initial discussion document, 2013)
- Appendix A – Values and Principles

Alistair Ponton

- Activity 2.3 – Initial Participation Audit
- Activity 2.6 – Advanced Participation Diagnostics

Natasha Ridley-Duff

- Activities 2.1 – 2.7 – Social Auditing / Diagnostics

Cliff Southcombe

- The FairShares Model (initial discussion document, 2013)
- Model Rules for a FairShares Company

Viewpoint Research CIC

- Activity 2.3 – Initial Participation Audit
- Activity 2.6 – Advanced Participation Diagnostics

Rory Ridley-Duff has asserted his right to be identified as the author of this work in accordance with the Copyright, Designs and Patents Acts 1988. First published in July 2015 by the author to members of the FairShares Association.

The author and the FairShares Association publish this book as a joint project: at least fifty percent of net revenues will be reinvested in the FairShares Association website and learning materials.

FairShares Association, 4 Rose Hill Close, Penistone, Sheffield, S36 6UF, United Kingdom

ISBN 13: 978-1512377668
ISBN 10: 151237766X

The Case for FairShares

www.fairshares.coop

http://creativecommons.org/licenses/by-nc-nd/4.0/

The general public can copy, distribute, display and perform this work if:

1. Original authors are given appropriate credit and a link is provided to the licence (Attribution)
2. Neither the work as a whole nor the rights in it are sold for commercial gain (Non-Commercial)
3. Any altered, transformed or built upon version of this work is not distributed (No Derivative Works)

Cover images provided by the FairShares Association.

FairShares Logo designed by Lam Vu Phuong Thinh.

Rory Ridley-Duff

The association for multi-stakeholder cooperation in member-owned social enterprises

Imagine a network of associations, cooperatives and companies where the knowledge creation model of Wikipedia is combined with the governance model of the John Lewis Partnership and the values and principles of the cooperative movement? This is a proxy for the FairShares Model. It is an approach that contributes to a society in which every adult can become a member-owner of the organisation(s) for which they work, from which they regularly buy goods and from which they receive social services.

In short, it envisages a society in which every adult becomes a co-owner of the organisations on which they, their family and their community depend.

Table of Contents

Using This Resource — 1
   Who initiated the FairShares Model? — 3

Part 1 – The Need for Change — 4
   The rise of solidarity cooperatives — 5
      Collective interests in the co-operative movement — 6
      Social entrepreneurship — 13
   New cooperativism and the FairShares Model — 16
   The case for FairShares — 23
      The key issue — 25
      Private sector (for-profit) norms — 26
      Voluntary sector (non-profit) norms — 27
      Social economy norms — 28
   The FairShares Model v2.x — 31
      Who is FairShares for? — 32
      Some limitations — 38
      How does a FairShares enterprise evolve? — 38
      Phase 1 – Informal democracy — 40
      Phase 2 – Embryonic democratic model — 42
      Phase 3 – Social democracy / cooperative governance — 44
      How do shareholders access wealth? — 45
   How can these ideas be applied to practice? — 47
      Application in worker-owned enterprises — 47
      Application in user-owned enterprises — 48
      Application in a cooperative consortium — 49
      How to convert to a FairShares association — 50
      How to convert to a FairShares company — 52
      Converting member-*controlled* cooperatives — 54
      Converting member-*owned* cooperatives — 55
      How to convert between legal forms — 56
   Where (exactly) did these ideas come from? — 57
   Conclusions — 61
   References — 64
      Key Working Papers on FairShares — 70

Part 2 – Educating for Change — 72
  Summary of learning activities — 73
  Activity 2.1 – Your social enterprise values — 74
    Guidance — 74
    Questions — 80
  Activity 2.2 – Level 1 social audit — 80
    Question — 82
  Activity 2.3 – Level 1 participation audit — 82
    Question — 85
  Activity 2.4 – Level 1 governance audit — 86
    Entrepreneurialism — 87
    Managerialism — 87
    Co-operative entrepreneurship — 88
    Stakeholder Democracy — 88
    Using the initial governance audit — 89
    Question — 90
  Activity 2.5 – Advanced management diagnostics — 91
    Guidance — 91
    Questions — 97
  Activity 2.6 – Advanced participation diagnostics — 97
    Guidance — 97
    Questions — 104
  Activity 2.7 – Advanced governance diagnostics — 105
  Activity 2.8 - Reviewing governance diagnostics — 107
    Questions — 108
  Activity 2.9 - Using FairShares to end exploitation — 108
  Activity 2.10 - Combatting wealth inequality — 109
  Activity 2.11 – Role play: taking big decisions — 109
    Future Energy Ltd — 109
    The proposal to members of Future Energy Ltd — 111
    Guidance to shareholders — 112
    Activity details — 113
    Distance learning guidance — 113
  Activity 2.12 - Building a solidarity enterprise — 115
  Activity 2.13 - Building a FairShares curriculum — 116

Part 3 – Instituting Change — 122
  Model rules version 2.1, 1st July 2015 — 125
    Model Rules for a FairShares Company — 126
    Model Rules for a FairShares Cooperative — 148

Model Rules for a FairShares Association	170
Appendix A – Values and Principles	**189**
Brand guidelines	189
Introduction	189
Brand principles	189
Levels of alignment	190
Brand variants	191
Brand identity	192
Brand values and social auditing	192
Appendix B - Resources	**193**
The Dragons' Apprentice: a social enterprise novel	193

Rory Ridley-Duff

Using This Resource

This book has been licensed to the FairShares Association by Rory Ridley-Duff under a Creative Commons 4.0 Licence. It contains works that have been reedited for this volume to form an integrated resource for researchers and educators who are creating learning and teaching resources for people learning about FairShares.

FairShares Articles of Association (and other documents referred to in this document) can be shared and adapted for your own use. In some cases they can be adapted for commercial use[1], providing the copyright notice and acknowledgements appear in the adapted versions and they are made available under a Creative Commons Licence formatted as follows.

© [IP Author 1], [IP Author 2] and
FairShares Association Ltd, 2014
Creative Commons 4.0: Attribution, Share Alike

If you upload any FairShares documentation to a website, cut/paste the following code to display the appropriate copyright notice and attributions:

---

[1] Fees may apply.

The Case for FairShares

```
<a rel="license" href="http://creativecommons.org/licenses/by-
sa/4.0/deed.en_GB"><img alt="Creative Commons Licence" style="border-width:0"
src="http://i.creativecommons.org/l/by-sa/4.0/88x31.png" /></a><br /><span
xmlns:dct="http://purl.org/dc/terms/" property="dct:title">The FairShares
Model</span> by <span xmlns:cc="http://creativecommons.org/ns#"
property="cc:attributionName">The FairShares Association</span> is licensed
under a <a rel="license" href="http://creativecommons.org/licenses/by-
sa/4.0/deed.en_GB">Creative Commons Attribution-ShareAlike 4.0 Unported
License</a>.
```

No warranty is provided that the contents of this book are suitable for your situation. They are provided to stimulate and inform innovation in the social and solidarity economy, to inform emerging practice, and to stimulate new thinking about the how to bring democratic management, ownership and governance into the heart of the social enterprise movement.

Professional advice is recommended if you are adapting the *FairShares Model* to your specific needs and circumstances. You can join the Online Community of the FairShares Association to discuss your needs with other professionals engaged with FairShares. The Online Community can organise access to:

- editable versions of model rules;
- financial forecasting spreadsheets;
- access to IP in a members' DropBox that may not be directly available to you;
- editing rights to the FairShares Wiki.
- Additional articles / news items on the FairShares Website.

Who initiated the FairShares Model?

Rory Ridley-Duff is Reader in Cooperative and Social Enterprise, and chair of the Principles of Responsible Management Group at Sheffield Business School. He was a founding subscriber of Social Enterprise London (1998) before studying for a doctorate (2002-5). In 2008, he began writing *Understanding Social Enterprise: Theory and Practice* for Sage Publications with Mike Bull (now regarded as the world's "first authoritative textbook" on social enterprise). In 2014, he authored *The Dragons' Apprentice* (CreateSpace), the "world's first social enterprise novel". He has written 35 scholarly articles and papers include a chapter on social economy for a United Nations' textbook *Principles of Responsible Management* (Cengage).

Cliff Southcombe is managing director of Social Enterprise Europe Ltd, a development agency that has operated for over 20 years from the north of England. In addition to delivering courses at Hull and Sheffield Hallam Universities, Cliff has an international profile through project work for the British Council and European Union. He was twice a director of Euclid, a European network of Third Sector leaders, and is currently a board member of the North East Social Enterprise Partnership.

Rory and Cliff are directors of Social Enterprise Europe Ltd. They co-founded the FairShares Association Ltd with Nicola Dickins (Make It Happen Consultancy Ltd) and Steve Wagstaff (Co-operative Group, South Yorkshire and Chesterfield Region).

The FairShares Model was published as a by-product of an award-winning paper by Rory and Cliff. They won 'Top Research and Knowledge Transfer Paper in Conference' at the 34th Institute of Small Business and Entrepreneurship (ISBE) Conference in 2011 for a paper called *Social Enterprise Mark: a critical review of its conceptual dimensions*. This was published in Volume 8, Issue 3 of the Social Enterprise Journal.

Part 1 – The Need for Change

In Part 1, I have threaded together arguments from a key note conference address, two short articles and a discussion document. These have been integrated to make the 'Case for FairShares'. The source materials are:

- *Solidarity Co-operatives* - presented at the RMIT Social Innovation and Research Colloquium (Melbourne) in November 2014 (co-authored with Mike Bull).
- *New Cooperativism and the FairShares Model* - first published in STIR Magazine, Vol 7 during 2014.
- *The Case for FairShares* - first published by the FairShares Association in early 2014.
- *The FairShares Model* - first published in February 2013, and subsequently updated for the 2014 and 2015 FairShares Association Conferences.

Each source has been re-edited to improve the quality of the underlying scholarship. New material has been added where appropriate.

The rise of solidarity cooperatives

This introduction examines the antecedents of the *FairShares Model* – an approach to creating solidarity co-operatives[2] that integrates the interests of founders, producers, consumers and small investors. In doing so, I outline an answer to the question "how has the concept of a 'solidarity co-operative' developed in the UK's social enterprise movement?" This is motivated by an interest in the way 'new co-operativism', and its focus on solidarity co-operatives, disrupts the logic of the common bond in 'old co-operativism'.[3]

By tracking the antecedent works of contributors to the *FairShares Model* between 1978 and 2013,[4] a (hidden) history of the social enterprise movement is revealed. This 'new co-operativism'[5] is part of an emerging social and solidarity economy that departs from 'old co-operativism' by regarding the common bond as something that is actively forged through acts of solidarity. This introduction, therefore, contributes to knowledge by clarifying the historical shifts that have led to the emergence of a social and solidarity economy, and how those shifts are now being expressed in the UK.

The *FairShares Model*, as presented by the FairShares Association,[6] comprises a set of brand principles, social auditing tools, management diagnostics and choice of model rules for 'self-governing co-operatives, mutuals and social enterprises' consistent with an international definition of social enterprise.[7] I retrieved documentation created by the

---

[2] Lund, 'Solidarity as a Business Model'.
[3] Compare Parnell, 'Co-operation – The Beautiful Idea' with Davies-Coates, 'Open Co-ops'.
[4] Prior to the formation of the FairShares Association.
[5] Vieta, 'The new co-operativism'; Davies-Coates, 'Open Co-ops'.
[6] FairShares Association Conference, 1st July 2014, Sheffield
[7] http://www.socialenterpriseeurope.co.uk/what-is-social-enterprise/ accessed 24th May 2015.

association up to May 2013[8] to examine how its founder members' commitment to "multi-stakeholder co-operation in member-owned social enterprises" was influenced over time.[9]

Collective interests in the co-operative movement

Robert Owen is identified as the person who shaped early developments in cooperative principles and his followers developed both producer and consumer cooperatives. He lived from 1771 - 1858 and rose to prominence through the creation of cooperative communities at New Lanark and New Harmony.[10] Owen was regarded by Karl Marx and Frederick Engels as 'utopian' for believing that poverty and inequality could be replaced by cooperative societies within a 'prosperous and harmonious community'.[11] After some limited successes in the UK and US, Owen's writings on the formation of character through educational and working practices were overshadowed by the writings of Marx and Engels. However, Owen's works formed an important strand of communitarian thought that resurfaced in later projects to build cooperative communities.[12]

Owen inspired the Rochdale Pioneers (to whom the Co-operative Group and the International Co-operative Alliance

---

[8] This is possible because the association's policy of publishing all its documentation with a Creative Commons Licence.
[9] The strapline was agreed by its members and supporters on *Loomio.org*, Sept 2014. For evidence of application see http://www.fairshares.coop.
[10] Owen, 'A New Vision of Society'. For reflections on Robert Owen, see Robertson, 'Robert Owen and the Campbell Debt' and Cooke, 'Robert Owen and the Stanley Mills'.
[11] Marx and Engels, 'The Communist Manifesto'; Balnave and Patmore, 'Rochdale consumer co-operatives in Australia', p. 986.
[12] Harrison, 'Robert Owen and the Owenites in Britain and America'; Rothschild and Allen-Whitt, 'The Co-operative Workplace'; Whyte and Whyte, 'Making Mondragon'.

trace their history). Charles Howarth, the author the first Laws and Objects of the Rochdale Society of Equitable Pioneers, and James Daly - the society's first secretary - were leaders of the 'Owenites' in Rochdale.[13] Rochdale Principles, however, go *beyond* Owen's vision of productive cooperation within an educated working class to more fundamental reforms based on one-person, one-vote principles. They also advanced a new arrangement for sharing surpluses based on individual payments that reflected production and consumption activity. The 1944 film about *The Rochdale Pioneers*, based on George Holyoake's histories, portrays Charles Howarth as the person who discovered the innovation of dividend payments in proportion to trading.[14]

Abbie Cathcart notes that Owen influenced John Spedan Lewis (JSL)[15] who sought to create his own 'cooperative society of producers' in the 1930s. In this endeavour, he made 'partnership' a more important principle than 'employment' to encourage a culture of sharing gains, information and power.[16] JSL spoke out vehemently against both nationalisation (which he regarded as a pathway to soviet-style communism) and a private economy of "absentee-capitalists who [get] excessive reward for their function of saving and lending".[17] Following bitter arguments with his father,[18] JSL argued that owners should

---

[13] Wilson, Shaw and Lonergan, 'Our Story: Rochdale Pioneers Museum'.
[14] Holyoake, 'Self-Help by the People' and 'The History of Co-operation'.
[15] Lewis, 'Partnership for All' and 'Fairer Shares' cited in Cathcart, 'Directing Democracy'.
[16] Lewis, 'Fairer Shares' (Part 1).
[17] Lewis, 'Partnership for All', p. 173, cited in Cathcart, 'Directing Democracy'.
[18] Cathcart, 'Directing Democracy'. She highlights an argument after JSL's father drew a dividend larger than the annual wage bill for his 300 staff.

not receive more compensation than the professionals they hire to run companies.[19]

The John Lewis Partnership (JLP) is now frequently cited as a model for both private and public sector reform.[20] Following the transfer of ownership to the workforce, staff joined and became 'partners' and beneficiaries of an Employee Benefit Trust (EBT). It was the Chair of the EBT, rather than individual workers, who owned the shares in John Lewis Department Stores and Waitrose until the formation of a trust company. Initially some partners held shares, but over time the trust acquired them and partners received profit-shares through the trust rather than individual dividend payments based on capital holdings.[21] The constitution permitted the workforce to elect 80% of the Partnership Council responsible for social development, and 40% of the board responsible for commercial decisions. As a Trust owned enterprise, JLP technically became a *commonly owned* enterprise, but its governance and management systems are underpinned by assumptions that pluralise the governing process through the negotiation of political interests and circular self-organising principles. Matrix management structures and dual reporting are embraced to create a cooperative culture. Membership principles rather than employment contracts are the primary guide to how relationships will develop between staff.[22]

---

[19] Paranque and Willmott, 'Co-operatives: saviours or grave-diggers of capitalism?' and Lewis, 'Fairer Shares'.
[20] A Google search for the term 'John Lewis Economy' (exact match) yielded 66,600 hits, while the terms 'John Lewis State' (exact match) yielded 730,000 hits on 1st July 2013.
[21] Spedan-Lewis, 'Fairer Shares'.
[22] Erdal, 'Beyond the Corporation'; Ridley-Duff, 2012a, 'New frontiers in self-management'.

The Co-operative Retail Society (now part of the Co-operative Group),[23] in contrast, developed a system of individual membership based on Rochdale Principles (formalised in 1957). Unlike John Lewis, UK consumer cooperatives adhered to the tradition of members providing share capital. However, many societies have not updated the value of early shareholdings. The £1 share contribution paid today is worth less than 1/500th the contribution of cooperative shareholders in 1844.[24] As cooperative societies (both consumer and worker owned) were initiated by member contributions, they were *jointly owned* enterprises that created both individual and cooperative capital[25] for members and divided it between individually owned member accounts and commonly owned capital reserves.

Rochdale Principles and Owen's interest in producer cooperation were important to Fr. Arizmendi at Fagor.[26] Arizmendi is credited with co-creating the Mondragon cooperatives with his students in the Basque region of Spain.[27] He drew on Owen's writings about education and the Rochdale Principles of one-person, one-vote and surplus sharing.[28] In adapting them, Mondragon's founders developed single stakeholder industrial (worker)

---

[23] Created out of the merger of the Co-operative Wholesale Society and Co-operative Retail Society in 2000.
[24] See Toms, 'Producer co-operatives and economic efficiency' for evidence of widespread working class ownership of producer co-ops in North West England. The Rochdale Pioneers Museum contain evidence that weekly wages dropped below £1 prior to 1844. A £1 share cost more than most members' weekly wage. In April 2013, the ONS estimated the median weekly salary in the UK was £517.
[25] Brown, 'Equity finance for social enterprises'.
[26] Molina, 'Fagor Eletricodomésticos'.
[27] BBC, 'The Mondragon Experiment', 17th November 1980, BBC Horizon Series.
[28] Whyte and Whyte, 'Making Mondragon'; Birchall, 'A member-owned business approach'.

cooperatives and solidarity cooperatives in banking, retailing and education.[29] Fagor, as outlined by Molina,[30] was instigated by Arizmendi to reinforce Christian ideals for a new entrepreneurial order that valued work over capital, and solidarity between workers and the wider community. The amounts invested by - and distributed to - individual members were much higher than the Co-operative Group. Nevertheless, the system retained the cooperative principle of member contributions, interest on capital and an entitlement to a share of surpluses. However, at Mondragon, member's initial capital contributions are divided: 20% goes to an indivisible reserve while the other 80% is retained in personal accounts. This system of *joint ownership* (in personal accounts) and *common ownership* (in collective funds) result in a socially liberal form of communitarianism. It reinforces individuals' interest in exercising their 'voice' in governing bodies whilst delegating some decision-making power to elected officials.

It is the evolution of systems for promoting solidarity at Mondragon (particularly in banking, retailing and education) that was significant to the later development of solidarity cooperatives. After 1960, a community bank (Caja Laborale) provided capital for new cooperative enterprises by raising funds from the local community (until neo-liberal banking reforms required them to diversity sources of capital).[31] While John Lewis and Mondragon's industrial cooperatives were employee-owned, and the Cooperative Retail Societies were consumer-owned, the Caja had features of both. Alex Bird (Wales Co-operative Centre) reports that a sophisticated system for joint worker and consumer

---

[29] Ridley-Duff, 2010, 'Communitarian corporate governance'.
[30] Molina, 'Fagor Domésticos'.
[31] Bird, 'Co-operation and Business Services'.

membership developed.[32] Governing councils elected both worker and consumer representatives.[33] Within the bank, the distribution of surpluses to workers was designed to encourage solidarity in another way: it was based on the profitability of the bank's cooperative business customers, not on the profitability of the bank itself.[34]

The models of solidarity at Mondragon represented an early intersection between communitarian philosophy and pluralism in ownership, governance and management, and this cooperative model was first communicated to an English-speaking audience through Oakeshott's book on worker co-operation in 1978.[35] The application of these pluralist principles at Mondragon resulted in business models with both indivisible *cooperative capital* and divisible *member capital*, accompanied by a wider distribution of capital and higher levels of democratic participation.[36] In front-line cooperatives (banking, retailing, education) multi-stakeholder principles were applied to ownership and governance. Even in single-stakeholder industrial cooperatives, the governance system is pluralised by having management, social and governing councils within *each* firm.

---

[32] Bird, 'Co-operation and Business Services'. In a personal communication on 24th June 2013 after reading Alex's book chapter on Mondragon in a Co-operative and Mutuals Wales publication, he confirmed that by 2013, 43% of the bank was worker-owned, and 57% consumer owned.

[33] Based on field notes collected by Rory Ridley-Duff during a field visit on 5th/6th March 2003. During the trip, it was explained by Mikel Lezamiz that workers were more interested in long term planning, justifying their presence on the board.

[34] Whyte and Whyte, 'Making Mondragon'; Davidmann, 'Co-op Study 7', http://www.solhaam.org/articles/mondra.html.

[35] Oakeshott, 'The Case for Worker Co-operatives'.

[36] Restakis, 'Humanising the Economy'. He reports that Italian co-operative limit worker ownership (often to around 20% of the workforce) ostensibly to limit the influence of the Mafia. At Mondragon, membership by workers is typically above 80%.

The Need for Change

Firms are 'member-owned', not 'investor-owned', committed to socialisation[37] rather than privatisation (Table 1.1) by ensuring that capital holdings and dividends are widely dispersed and based on members' activities.

Table 1.1 – Privatisation v Socialisation

	Privatisation (creating 'unjust' equilibria)	Socialisation (create 'just' equilibria)
Key characteristic	The acquisition of public/social rights by private individuals/corporations to bring capital** under private (management) control.	The sharing of public/social rights among groups representing primary stakeholders* so they can jointly control an enterprise's capital.
Human / Intellectual capital	Traditional Copyright Law, Encyclopaedia Britannica, Patents	Creative Commons, Wikipedia, Open Source Software
Intellectual property management	Acquisition of rights to fully formed ideas and designs created by producers / employees so they can be commercially exploited (or removed from the market).	Distribution and / or sharing of fully formed ideas so that producers can use and exchange them in new creative works (and prevent their removal from the market).
Social capital	Marks & Spencer (Europe), IBM (US), Foxconn (China)	John Lewis (Europe), MindValley (Asia), SEMCO (South America)
Governance and control	Exclusion of primary stakeholders from governance/audit (except as information providers); accountability of stakeholders to executive management / private owners.	Equal participation of primary stakeholders in governance and audit; accountability of executives to primary stakeholders through elected governing bodies or statutory requirements

---

[37] For a comparison of privatisation, socialisation and nationalisation see Ridley-Duff, 2012a, 'New frontiers in self-management'.

Natural capital	Private monopoly control of natural resources (e.g. British Gas, Bechtel Corporation)	Co-operative and community energy projects (e.g. Denmark, Germany, Africa)
Resource management	Individual / corporate control of natural capital by corporate managers; commercial exploitation of 'common pool resources' (water, air, minerals, etc.)	Co-operative / mutual group control of natural resources by stewards and users; micro producer-consumer enterprises (e.g. home owners producing and consuming their own electricity)
Financial capital	Arsenal FC, Holland & Barrett, Enron	Barcelona FC, Suma Wholefoods, SEMCO
Ownership	Individual or corporate control over membership; shares issued in exchange for financial capital	Open membership / capital rights for primary stakeholders; shares issued in exchange for labour / consumer participation

Source: *Understanding Social Enterprise: Theory and Practice (2nd edn.)*, Table 10.4

Copyright 2015, Rory Ridley-Duff and Mike Bull, Creative Commons 4.0 Licence, BY-NC-SA

* Primary stakeholders = employees, producers, customers and/or service users

** Capital = human/intellectual, social, financial and natural

There is, however, another trajectory in history that we need to consider if we are to understand the intellectual antecedents of the *FairShares Model*. This comes from the conscious effort of founders and worker-owners engagement in entrepreneurship that has a positive impact on the well-being of people and the environment. In the next section, we consider how this has led to the field of social entrepreneurship and the emergence of social enterprise as a business concept.

Social entrepreneurship

Since the early 1990s, entrepreneurial action in pursuit of social goals has been actively developed as an academic discipline.[38] Alvord *et al*, argue that social entrepreneurship has been theorised in a multitude of ways: as business practices that make social organisations viable;[39] as action that improves the well-being of marginalized communities,[40] and as the reconfiguration of existing resources to improve welfare.[41] Recently, more focus has been placed on the value propositions of social entrepreneurs,[42] the 'shared value' they create[43] and the social innovations that sustain them.[44]

Whilst the US discourse is frequently linked to Muhammad Yunus' notion of private sector support for entrepreneurially driven social businesses, Yunus himself identified a 'second type' that marries community action with a cooperative model of ownership and control. This model of solidarity and co-operation is designed to ensure that "social benefit is derived from the fact that dividends and equity growth...benefit the poor, thereby helping them to reduce their poverty or even escape it altogether".[45] Significantly, it was the *second* model, and not the first, that underpinned the Grameen Bank in 1976[46] (a project that led to Yunus winning a Nobel Prize in 2008). This consumer-owned bank is now owned by its producer members. The bank lends money to members to fund their production (not

---

[38] Harvard University established its social enterprise initiative in 1993.
[39] Alvord *et al.,* 'Social entrepreneurship and societal transformation'; Emerson and Twerksy, 'New Social Entrepreneurs'.
[40] Dees, 'Enterprising non-profits'; Nicholls, 'Social Entrepreneurship'.
[41] Uphoff, 'Reasons for Success'.
[42] Martin and Osberg, 'Social entrepreneurship: the case for definition'; Chell, 'Social enterprise and entrepreneurship'.
[43] Porter and Kramer, 'Creating shared value'.
[44] Perrini and Vurco, 'Social entrepreneurship: innovation and social change'; Nicholls and Murdock, 'Social Innovation'.
[45] Yunus, 'Creating a World without Poverty', Kindle edition (at 14%, "Two Kinds of Social Businesses").
[46] Jain, 'Managing credit for the rural poor: lessons from the Grameen Bank'.

their consumption) activities. In this way it mirrors the logic of the Caja Laborale at Mondragon, but at a micro rather than a mezzo or macro level.[47]

Robert Owen, the Rochdale Pioneers, John Spedan Lewis, Fr. Arizmendi (and those that followed them) also engaged in the creation of 'second type' social businesses by using knowledge of entrepreneurship and ownership arrangements instrumentally to ensure that dividends and equity were spread widely throughout the communities on which they depended. Their social entrepreneurship is expressed through social innovations in the constitution of organisations to secure solidarity and well-being for founders, producers, consumers and small investors. Indeed, their work reframes who a 'primary stakeholder' is by redefining the role and rights of capital, membership criteria, and the arrangements for decision-making.

However, we cannot complete this early history without integrating the work of Jaroslav Vanek.[48] He argued that Yugoslav[49] labour-*managed* firms bridged a social divide by removing the incentive for managers to distance themselves socially from production workers. The logic of Vanek's argument is used to explain the achievements at Mondragon and John Lewis (see Ellerman,[50] Turnbull[51] and Erdal[52]). They

---

[47] At Mondragon, money was lent by members of the community to fund production in industrial worker co-operatives (often at scale). In contrast, the loans at the Grameen Bank initially funded individual or household production. The logic, however, is similar. Producers owned the bank (as consumers of the bank's services).

[48] Vanek, 'The General Theory of Labor-Managed Market Economies', cited in Ridley-Duff, Southcombe and Dickins, 2013.

[49] After the Yugoslav wars, Yugoslavia divided into: Croatia, Slovenia, Macedonia, Bosnia and Herzegovina and the Federal Republic of Yugoslavia (Serbia). In 2006, Montenegro separated from Serbia.

[50] Ellerman, 'Entrepreneurship in the Mondragon Co-operatives' and 'The Democratic Worker-Owned Firm'.

each argue that removing the employment relationship (within the firm) undermining the mechanism by which labour is impoverished. The idea of a market economy in which firms are organised as member-owned enterprises is a key departure from existing norms in the private, public and charity sectors. Moreover, Golja and Novkovic state that the arrangements in the former Yugoslavia oriented its social economy toward a *multi*-stakeholder model, not the single-stakeholder model popularised in Anglo-American settings. This being that case, there are a multitude of arguments developing for cooperatives to provide a "platform for multi-stakeholder participation (workers, producers, sellers and buyers)" to improve the sustainability of business.[53]

In Figure 1.1, I summarise the interpretation of these findings to show how consumer, worker and solidarity cooperatives represent different strands of development within the wider cooperative movement. It is the bringing together of these different strands during the 1970s that created the conditions for 'new co-operativism' to emerge.

New cooperativism and the FairShares Model

In July 2014, Cliff Southcombe and Rory Ridley-Duff met Margaret Meredith and Catalina Quiroz, the organisers of a three-year project to develop education resources for the social economy at York St John University. Margaret and Catalina had been travelling in South America for three months to learn about the solidarity economy. Cliff and Rory had met them initially at the FairShares Association Conference, then again at the Cooperative and Social

---

[51] Turnbull, 'Stakeholder democracy', 'Innovations in corporate governance' and 'A New Way to Govern'.
[52] Erdal, 'The Psychology of Sharing' and 'Beyond the Corporation'.
[53] Golja and Novkovic, 'Determinants of cooperative development in Croatia', p. 21; Novkovic and Webb, 'Co-ops in a Post-Growth Era'.

Enterprise Summer School hosted by Sheffield Hallam University. After four days of discussion, they told me that they wanted to include the *FairShares Model* in a handbook on new cooperativism. This got me thinking about what's new about the *FairShares Model* and its relationship to old cooperativism.

Figure 1.1 – Historical influences on FairShares

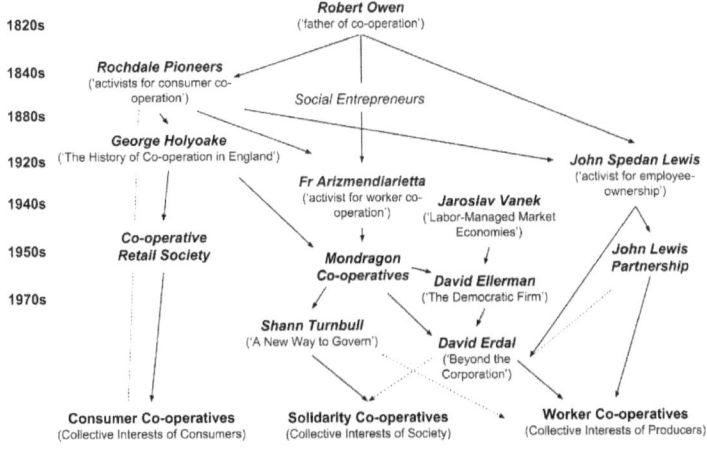

Copyright 2014, Rory Ridley-Duff and Mike Bull, Creative Commons 4.0 Licence, BY-NC-SA

The *FairShares Model* is a project of Social Enterprise Europe. In this agency, the board recognised that the earliest developments in social enterprise between 1976 to 1982 were rooted in commitments to cooperative values and principles: social finance at the Grameen Bank, Bangladesh (1976); social auditing at Beechwood College, Leeds, UK (1978); social cooperatives in Bologna, Italy (1978), and — the exception — social entrepreneurship that developed at Ashoka (USA, 1982). Each initiative developed contributions to practice that we take for granted today. Importantly, they supported projects that combined member ownership with sustainable development goals that maximised social impact. Even at Unilever, the Chief Operating Officer

The Need for Change

Harish Manwani now argues that there is an inexorable move towards a 'responsible business' model in which a licence to operate should be granted only when an enterprise can show that it creates both economic and social value.[54]

Cliff's first formal encounter with social enterprise took place at the Social Enterprise Partnership (1994) and my own came at Social Enterprise London (in 1997). In the 1990s, groups of people involved in worker cooperatives forged alliances with their cooperative development agencies, a cooperative college and advocates of sustainable development to forge new thinking. Cliff co-founded The Social Enterprise Partnership which went on to become Social Enterprise Europe Ltd. He published the 2nd Edition of the *Social Audit Toolkit* with Freer Spreckley in 1997. Rory was one of the initial subscribers to Social Enterprise London (SEL). The first social enterprise degree was created with SEL's support at the University of East London (in 2001). It also initiated the Social Enterprise Journal (in 2005). In 2012, after the UK government withdrew funding from the sector, SEL decided to merge with Social Enterprise UK.

There was considerable experimentation going on at that time: Poptel created a corporate structure to attract venture capital, but later had to transfer part of itself to the Phone Coop after losing control to Sun International; Computercraft (Rory's employer) held extensive discussions with Gavin Boby of Democratic Business Ltd on how to combine cooperative shares (for voting) with ordinary shares (to represent the wealth invested and created by members); and David Erdal was also based in London back then, turning Robert Oakeshott's Job Ownership Ltd into today's Employee Ownership Association.

---

[54] Manwani, 'Profit's not always the point', http://www.ted.com/talks/harish_manwani_profit_s_not_always_the_point?language=en, accessed 24th May 2015.

With hindsight, it's possible to see these examples as some of the social incubation hotspots of new cooperativism. Before the late 1990s, worker ownership in the UK was dominated by an interpretation of Rochdale Principles at the *Industrial Common Ownership Movement*, based on a £1 membership fee (ignoring that £1 in 1844 was the equivalent to about £500 today). Unlike early cooperatives that paid as much as 10p in the £1 as a dividend, reward systems became more based on wages. David Erdal, like myself, had visited the Mondragon Cooperatives where workers invest up to 15% of their first year salary on membership and receive up to 70% of surpluses as credits to a cooperative bank account.[55] Democratic Business Ltd — created by Guy Major and Gavin Boby — also expected investments by the workforce. They designed a system for issuing voting shares for labour contributions and profit shares for financial contributions with an ingenious mechanism for 'value added sharing'[56] amongst stakeholders based on share issues rather than bonus payments. As at Mondragon, this was designed to increase working capital and reduce the cost of making new investments. From 1999 to 2012 (Figure 1.2) these ideas were mixed with ideas in model rules created by Geof Cox (Stakeholder Model, Common Cause Foundation), Morgan Killick (NewCo Model, ESP Projects Ltd) and myself (Surplus Sharing Model, for Social Enterprise Europe).[57] In 2012, these results were branded as the *FairShares Model* and the FairShares Association was created to support professional development and make intellectual property available to educators, consultants and social entrepreneurs

---

[55] Ridley-Duff, 'Communitarian Perspectives on Corporate Governance'.
[56] Major and Boby, 'Equity Devaluation'.
[57] These are three of the 'four important cases' described at http://www.fairshares.coop/wp-content/uploads/2014/11/Identities-and-Legalities-Cases.pdf.

The Need for Change

who want to create multi-stakeholder associations, cooperatives and companies.[58]

Founder shares[59] are issued for the entrepreneurial effort needed to bring an organisation into existence, and *Labour Shares* are issued to people engaged in production. This might be producers (in an agricultural/artisan cooperative) or employees (in a co-owned business). *User Shares* are issued to consumers who trade regularly with the enterprise or who are regular beneficiaries / users of its services. Lastly, *Investor Shares*[60] are issued to any person (natural or legal) contributing or creating patient capital. Many of these are destined to end up in the hands of producers and consumers because a FairShares constitution guarantees that half the capital gain is distributed as Investor Shares to recognise that capital is *created* by their interactions with each other.

Figure 1.2 – FairShares as a solidarity cooperative

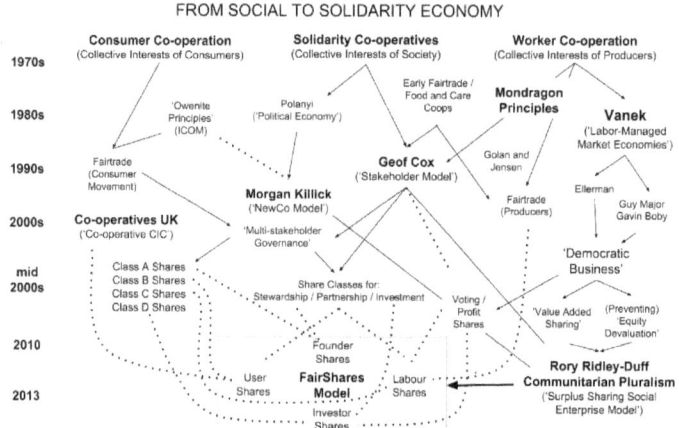

Copyright 2014, Rory Ridley-Duff and Mike Bull,
Creative Commons 4.0 Licence, BY-NC-SA

---

[58] Ridley-Duff and Bull, 'The FairShares Model: a communitarian pluralist approach'.
[59] In the association model of FairShares, memberships rather than shares are offered.
[60] Investor Shares are not offered in the association model.

In the previous epoch of cooperativism (from 1844 to 1978), the notion of a *common bond* was framed through the needs of a single stakeholder. As Edgar Parnell explains:

> *"Members of the common bond group are those the enterprise was established to serve...for example: in a consumer cooperative, the common bond will be that they are all consumers; in an agricultural cooperative, all are farmers; in a credit union or building society, all savers and borrowers; and in a tenants' housing cooperative, all are tenants."*[61]

The problem with this arrangement is that 'other' groups are then treated as subservient to the needs of those with a pre-defined common bond, producing destructive side-effects. For example, recognising that consumer cooperatives could treat labour in much the same way as other private sector employers, Peter Davis wrote a book on human resource management to help improve their labour relations.[62] Similarly, before crowd-funding and community share issues, cooperatives were frequently hostile to 'outside' investors.[63] Cooperation might — as Parnell claims — be a beautiful idea but it becomes ugly when it institutionalises a system of mutual distrust and ignores the common bond that is forged through joint action and shared experiences.

The limitations of old cooperativism, therefore, stem from an ongoing insistence that non-members must behave as philanthropists. The logic goes something like this, "Yes, you can work here so long as you accept that consumers come first" (i.e. that workers must be tacit philanthropists). Alternatively, "Yes, you buy from us so long as you accept that profits go to producers" (i.e. consumers must be tacit

---

[61] Parnell. 'Cooperation: The Beautiful Idea', p. 13.
[62] Davis, 'Human Resources Management in Co-operatives'.
[63] Ridley-Duff and Bull, 'Understanding Social Enterprise', 2nd Edition.

philanthropists). More recently, I've encountered the following attitude, "Yes, you can invest in us so long as you do not expect a return any time soon, if ever" (i.e. that community capital is seen as a quasi-donation rather than an investment choice).

New cooperativism (1978 – now) places more emphasis on a shared return and solidarity *between* stakeholders, and places less emphasis on meeting the needs of a *single* stakeholder. Marcelo Vieta highlights five characteristics:[64]

1. Responses by working people and grassroots groups to the crisis of neo-liberalism;
2. Innovations in meeting needs, uninhibited by pre-existing cooperative sentiments;
3. New approaches to wealth distribution that observe sustainable development constraints;
4. More horizontal labour relations, and more egalitarian schemes for allocating surpluses;
5. A stronger community orientation, with social objects and community development goals.

While guided by ICA Principles, Vieta looks to Kropotin's works to define new cooperativism as the:

> "...innumerable forms of collective economic practices and social values that are rooted in mutual aid amongst ourselves..."

The acceptance of multi-stakeholder cooperativism marks a substantial change: Josef Davies-Coates has recently called this an open cooperative movement,[65] and notes that Ed Mayo, General Secretary of Cooperatives UK, regards this as "an idea whose time has come." This model not only forges a common bond through the passive accident of a

---

[64] Vieta, 'The new co-operativism'.
[65] Davies-Coates, 'Open co-ops'. I followed up the comment attributed to Ed Mayo in person at the International Cooperative Summit in Quebec. Ed Mayo was comfortable with the attribution.

shared demographic or social characteristic, but also through acts of political activism. Italian social cooperatives actively integrated state, beneficiaries, workers and carers in pursuit of a more socially just care system.[66] As we noted earlier, Mondragon's Cooperative Bank (Caja Laborale) and retail chain (Eroski) integrated both worker and consumer members into their ownership and governance processes to aid socio-economic transformation.[67]

The *FairShares Model* articulates the case for integrating (social) entrepreneurs, producers, consumers and (social and community) investors. With these changes, the common bond is understood and experienced differently. Whilst it may pre-exist in a situation or shared characteristic, it also exists in the shared experience of creating alternatives to neo-liberalism. It is based on common bonds that emerge from the application of multi-stakeholder systems of ownership, governance and management to advance social enterprise development. The benefits sought and interests protected are different rather than the same, but the spirit of cooperation remains the same — to create an economy based on mutual aid rather than market competition.[68]

The case for FairShares

At the start of 2014, members of the FairShares Association came across new studies that acted as a powerful reminder of the need for a *FairShares Model*. In this section, I describe the most striking of these, then argue that the cooperative and social enterprise movements need to concern themselves with everyone in the 'bottom' 80% of the population, not just

---

[66] Restakis, 'Humanizing the Economy'; Borzaga and Depedri, 'When social enterprises do it better'.
[67] Whyte and Whyte, 'Making Mondragon'.
[68] Ridley-Duff and Bull, 'The FairShares Model: a communitarian pluralist approach'.

The Need for Change

those in extreme poverty. They also need to protect the wealth embedded in our natural environment.

In 2014, I was sent a link to a YouTube animation that portrays private wealth distribution in the US using data from a study at Harvard University.[69] This tells a completely different story to *Shift Change*,[70] a documentary about the social economy in the US and Spain. While the Harvard study reports that top US CEOs get **380** times the *average* worker's pay, *Shift Change* reports that worker cooperatives either adopt equal pay systems or accept small wage differentials sanctioned by the worker-owners. For example, the ratio between top and *lowest* paid workers in the Mondragon Coops – where there are 100,000 workers - averages just **5:1**.[71]

The animation based on the Harvard study claims that **90%** of citizens are now impoverished by private sector business practices. The 'bottom' 80% owns just 7% of total wealth, while the top 20% has 93%. Only 10% gain, and the top 1% gain disproportionately. There is no doubt that Hayek's theory that economic freedom leads to a 'trickle down' effect is untrue. It produces a 'trickle up' effect instead.[72] But *Shift Change* shows that where cooperative business models become dominant, wealth is spread more evenly and equitably. Member-owned businesses more often than not, are as (commercially) successful as their private sector counterparts.[73] That's where the *FairShares Model* comes in – it adds support for the growth of the social

---

[69] Norton, and Ariely, D. 'Building a better America'.
[70] Young and Dworkin 'Shift Change' (Film), www.shiftchange.org.
[71] Melman, 'After Capitalism'; Erdal, 'Beyond the Corporation'.
[72] Hayek, 'The Constitution of Liberty', 'Law, Legislation and Liberty'.
[73] Pérotin and Robinson, 'Employee Participation, Firm Performance and Survival'; Birchall, 'People-Centred Businesses'.

economy through the adoption of solidarity as a business model.[74]

The key issue

Most social enterprises focus on the poorest communities. Whilst important, it is *more urgent* that we reform systems that exploit and impoverish up to 90% of working people (as well as the environment in which they live). We need social enterprises for the bottom 90% (*everyone* impoverished) not just the bottom 10% (the *most* impoverished). We also need a way to prevent the top 10% of earners acquiring hegemonic control over investment decisions. If this task is beyond us, the goals of social enterprise will also be beyond us.

It is not an accident that most people are getting poorer (in both absolute and relative terms). Studies of company law make it clear than private enterprises are not designed to share power or wealth.[75] Founders fix structures at incorporation to privilege a set of interests (i.e. entrepreneur(s) and financial investors in companies, consumers or workers in single stakeholder cooperatives). Charitable organisations are also inflexible: board and workforce members assume they are subordinate to charitable/social objects set by the founders.[76]

Entrepreneurship research clarifies how enterprises start. One or more founding members - by design or accident – find opportunities to develop new markets for products and services.[77] If viable, they organise resources to support a business and build socio-technical systems to maintain management control. Growing enterprises, however, also depend on the goodwill of the workforce, customers (service

---

[74] Lund, M. 'Solidarity as a Business Model'.
[75] Davies, 'Introduction to Company Law'.
[76] Coule, 'Sustainability in Voluntary Organisations'.
[77] Chell, 'Social enterprise and entrepreneurship'.

users) and institutional investors to access the human, social and financial capital needed for sustainability.[78]

The **key issue** is that while we have developed systems for recognising the contribution of financial capital, we do not have adequate arrangements for recognising contributions of intellectual, human, social and natural capital. To understand why, we have to review the way social norms for constituting joint-stock companies and non-share companies have developed.[79]

Private sector (for-profit) norms

There is a connection between business ideology and the arrangements in law by which entrepreneurs acquire share capital (ordinary shares).[80] They register as directors, then recruit employees to operationalize their ideas. New capital is issued when more *financial* capital is needed, but not when more intellectual, human, social or natural capital are needed. In an unadapted CLS, employees and customers are subordinated to the interests of shareholders. They are not invited to be full members or to contribute towards decisions outside their specialist area of expertise.[81] If employees *are* offered share capital, voting rights are often limited or controlled by trustees who – in many cases – are under no legal obligation to vote in accordance with the *wishes* of their beneficiaries.[82]

The intellectual property created by the workforce is acquired by the Company and controlled by executive

---

[78] Coule, 'Sustainability in Voluntary Organisations'.
[79] McCulloch and Ridley-Duff, 'Beyond Accounting for Capitals: FairShares – a model for recompensing capital contributions'.
[80] Davies, 'An Introduction to Company Law'.
[81] Erdal, 'Beyond the Corporation'.
[82] Rodrick, 'Leveraged ESOPs and Employee Buyouts'.

managers and directors.[83] In effect, majority shareholders treat intellectual, human, social and natural capital investments by others as if they were additional *financial* investments by themselves. They continue to acquire rights to all the property created by the interactions between employees, customers and the natural environment. This system of enterprise widens the wealth gap between those who own and govern the enterprise, and those who sell their labour to it, or buy goods from it. Even in the richest countries, wealth inequalities grow wider (unless the state intervenes)[84] and the natural environment is degraded.[85]

Voluntary sector (non-profit) norms

A typical response to the social problems created by privately owned economies is to create (private) charities and 'non-profit' companies using a Company Limited by Guarantee (CLG). This form of incorporation usually involves specifying charitable or social objects that define the purpose(s) of the enterprise. Founders reframe themselves as trustee-directors responsible for allocating resources in pursuit of social goals.

Charitable CLGs do not issue share capital so trustee-directors give up personal rights to the surplus wealth created by the enterprise. Their role (in law) is one of stewardship, ensuring that funds raised are used to further charitable (or social) objectives defined in the Articles of Association. As in a CLS, they employ staff to pursue social goals. Employees are still not (usually) legal members. They continue to be subordinate to the trustee-directors and give up the (intellectual) property they create.

---

[83] Ridley-Duff and Bull, 'Understanding Social Enterprise', 2nd Edition, Chapter 12.
[84] Wilkinson and Pickett, 'The Spirit Level'.
[85] Hawken, 'The Ecology of Commerce'.

Social economy norms

Do we have to choose between these two models? Three bodies of knowledge suggest we do not. Firstly, there is a global movement backed by the UN to increase responsible use of corporate assets.[86] Secondly, the UN's International Year of Cooperatives highlighted the global growth of the social economy.[87] Particularly important is the way that the internet has reduced the costs associated with cooperative working. The upsides of cooperation (intellectual exchange and collaborative decision-making) no longer come with the downsides of democracy (hefty co-ordination costs).[88] Lastly, more enterprises identify themselves as *social*, deploying business models that improve human well-being through innovative trading strategies.[89]

Creating non-shareholding companies enables the wealthier sections of society to address some symptoms of poverty and exclusion that private enterprises create, but it cannot address the root causes because it changes neither the ownership structure nor governance processes that creates and sustains them. Traditional private / non-profit models continue to institutionalise a division between producers and consumers on the one hand, and entrepreneurs and (social) investors on the other. For this reason, Level 1 of the *FairShares Model* (Figure 1.3) asks important questions about representation in ownership, governance and management.

As shown in Figure 1.3, the *FairShares Model* is based on an approach to social economy defined by Social Enterprise Europe. It operates from the assumption that the exclusion of primary stakeholders from member-ownership (i.e.

---

[86] Laasch and Conway, 'Principles of Responsible Management'.
[87] ICA/Euricse, 'The World Co-operative Monitor'.
[88] Murray, 'Co-operation in the Age of Google'.
[89] Ridley-Duff and Bull, 'Understanding Social Enterprise'.

employees, producers, customers and service users) is a cause of contemporary poverty.

figure 1.3 – FairShares level 1 – initial social audit

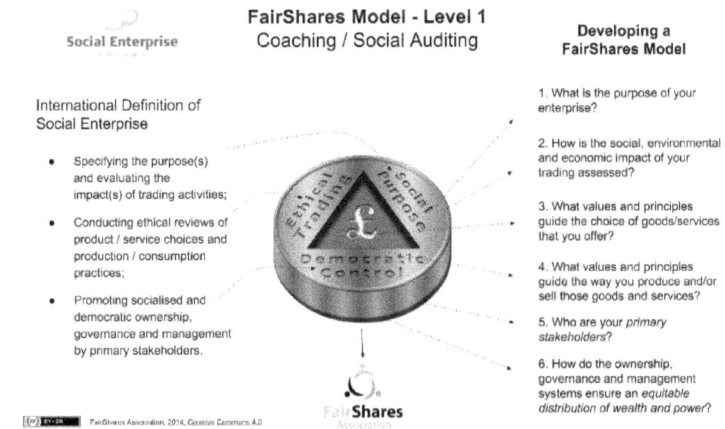

Copyright 2015, Rory Ridley-Duff
Creative Commons 4.0 Licence, BY-NC-SA

figure 1.4 – FairShares level 2 – design principles

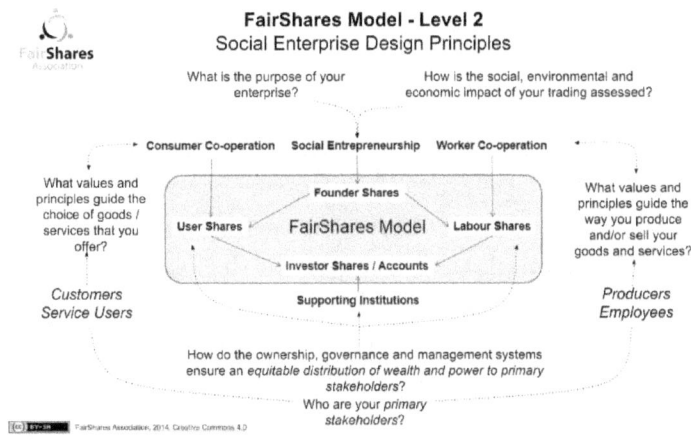

Copyright 2015, Rory Ridley-Duff
Creative Commons 4.0 Licence, BY-NC-SA

The Need for Change

At Level 2 (Figure 1.4), the answer to each FairShares question suggests the set of corporate arrangements that is most favourable: entrepreneurs get Founder Shares; workforce members get Labour Shares; trading commitments are rewarded with User Shares; and financial capital creation is rewarded with Investor Shares.

This represents a new approach to valuing investments. When there are surpluses (profits), not only do the providers of financial capital get a return, but also the contributors of other types of capital. In a FairShares Company, half the capital gain is issued to Labour and User Shareholders as *new* Investor Shares, while the other half increases the value of *existing* Investor Shares. In a FairShares Cooperative, surpluses can be allocated to restricted funds controlled by Labour and User member-owners, who then use their chosen approach to direct democracy to allocate surpluses to social investment projects.

None of this means that the conventional mechanism for allocating shares to external financial investors has to stop. In a FairShares Company / Cooperative, Investor Shares can be issued to external investors if debt finance is hard to secure. **But, even with this, at least 70% of the wealth accumulated will find its way into the hands (and bank balances) of producers and consumers.** It enriches the 'bottom' 90% as much as the 'top' 10%. And if this is not sufficient, FairShares Articles of Association (at Level 3) includes community dividends that act as an asset lock for philanthropic capital if the enterprise is dissolved.

The Articles of Association provided by the FairShares Association are not the only model rules that support *FairShares* values and principles.[90] But they do represent an ambitious attempt to bring together the most enduring

---

[90] See http://www.socentstructures.org.uk/, a new joint venture by Social Enterprise Europe, Geof Cox Associates and NESEP.

developments in multi-stakeholder ownership, governance and management so that we change the way investments are recognised and valued.[91] The *FairShares Model* offers a system for ensuring that capital is allocated to different types of contribution so that wealth and power can be more fairly shared.

The FairShares Model v2.x [92]

Imagine a network of associations, cooperatives and companies where the knowledge creation model of Wikipedia is combined with the governance model of the John Lewis Partnership and the values and principles of the cooperative movement? This is a proxy for the *FairShares Model*. It is an approach that contributes to a society in which every adult can become a member-owner of the organisation(s) for which they work, from which they regularly buy goods, and from which they receive social services. In short, it envisages a society in which every adult becomes a co-owner of the organisations on which they, their family and their community depend.

This section describes the *FairShares Model* in more detail. Association members are working with partner organisations in other countries (e.g. France, Germany, Croatia, Nigeria and Indonesia) to establish how this model can operate in any country that allows the registration of joint-stock companies and/or cooperatives with different

---

[91] Westall, 'Value-Led, Market-Driven'; Ridley-Duff, 'New frontiers in democratic self-management'.

[92] The first version of this document was agreed by Rory Ridley-Duff, Cliff Southcombe and Nicci Dickins in February 2013. It was updated by Rory Ridley-Duff in June 2014 and June 2015 for each FairShares Association Conference, see http://shura.shu.ac.uk/6635/ and http://shura.shu.ac.uk/8470/.

classes of share, and which provides for associations with different types of member.

The *FairShares Model* is more than an approach to creating associations, cooperatives and companies, it is also a methodology for social enterprise development that draws inspiration from cooperative values and principles. It comprises:

1. A set of values and principles (see Appendix A).
2. Tools for social auditing, learning and research;
3. Advanced management diagnostics;
4. Model rules for associations, cooperatives and companies;
5. A wiki with support documentation / information;
6. A membership organisation that connects practitioners, educators, consultants and researchers working together to investigate and develop the model;
7. Educational materials (included in this book) to help the above groups learn more about the concepts, principles and practices of FairShares.

In the pages that following, footnotes refer to clauses in FairShares Model Rules provided in Part 3 of this book.

Who is FairShares for?

The concept of a FairShares Enterprise will appeal to any person or organisation wishing to create (or support the creation of) self-governing associations, cooperatives and social enterprises. It will interest: cooperative members; cooperative development agencies; employee owned businesses; social entrepreneurs; cooperative and social enterprise consultants; community development workers; policy makers on economic regeneration; political parties; government bodies; mutual societies; and charities and private businesses that want to create social enterprises. It may also interest social investors and public authorities looking for models that support new approaches to patient equity in the social economy.

Central to the concept of a FairShares Enterprise – similar to experiments at the John Lewis Partnership - is power, information and wealth sharing. This makes it an excellent model for joint venture creation involving social, public and private bodies that want to create and deliver goods and services. It has a heritage rooted in innovations that led to a renaissance in cooperative and employee-owned businesses, particularly where power is shared amongst primary stakeholders.

This model will **not** be of interest to entrepreneurs seeking to accumulate and then privatise wealth (unless their medium/long-term goal is sharing that wealth with their workforce and wider community). It will not be attractive to financial investors / funders who require control rights and/or the privatisation of IP before making an investment.

A FairShares Enterprise addresses issues identified in *The Case for FairShares* by building in mechanisms from the outset to distribute intellectual, financial and social capital to the stakeholders who are needed to sustain it. Spreading power and wealth as it accumulates inhibits the emergence of unaccountable elites. It contributes to a society in which wealth and power is fairly shared.[93]

The *FairShares Model* achieves power and wealth sharing through the application of Cooperative Values and Principles within a social enterprise:

- *Governance processes recognise both individuals and interest groups, following (and extending) the 1st, 2nd and 3rd ICA cooperative principles of open membership, democratic member control and member economic participation.* Founders become members and have their participation rights in governance protected. Membership is then extended through Labour, User and Investor Shares (or Membership) to any natural or legal person

---

[93] Spedan-Lewis, 'Fairer Shares'.

who: a) continuously provides labour; b) continuously engages in trade; and c) is willing to invest patient capital. As share capital / membership is offered for entrepreneurial, intellectual, labour, trading and financial contributions, financial investment ceases to be the sole basis for offering membership. Personal rights replace property rights as the rationale for membership,[94] and group rights are balanced with individual rights to change power relations in governing bodies.[95]

- *Knowledge production and sharing processes create an intellectual commons with IP belonging to its creator(s) and licensed to associations, cooperatives or companies by their members. This implements ICA principles 4 - 7: autonomy and independence; member and public education; cooperation amongst cooperators/cooperatives; concern for community.* The Creative Commons Licence that enables knowledge sharing on Wikipedia also underpins the FairShares approach to IP. Members' IP is licensed by its creators to FairShares Enterprises using a Creative Commons licence. This ensures IP can be used by the enterprise and its members, but does not involve a transfer of ownership from the creator(s) to the enterprise. This has the effect of creating an intellectual commons while preventing the alienation of producers from the IP they create. If a member leaves, the IP can be used by both the creator(s) and the enterprise to which it was licensed.

Open membership is achieved by ensuring that qualifying contributions are fair and reasonable, and can be achieved by workforce members and users through their day-to-day trading / interaction with the enterprise (Table 1.2).

---

[94] Ellerman, 'The Democratic Worker-Owned Firm'.
[95] Ridley-Duff, 'New frontiers in democratic self-management'.

Table 1.2 – Share types[96]

Share Types	When are they issued?	When do they change value?	When are they cancelled?
Founder Shares (Members) Created at the inception of the enterprise	At incorporation only	Never	When a founder asks for them to be cancelled, or when they are forfeited on death, bankruptcy, insolvency or winding up.
Labour Shares (Members) Created when production work begins.	Issued when a provider of labour makes a qualifying contribution.	Never – but holding them determines the issue of investor shares and payment of dividends.	When the member no longer makes qualifying contributions (e.g. on the termination of an agreement to provide labour, upon death, bankruptcy, insolvency or winding up).
User Shares (Members) Created when trading activities begin.	Issued when a user or consumer makes a qualifying contribution.	Never – but holding them determines the issue of investor shares and payment of dividends.	When the member no longer makes a qualifying contribution (e.g. on the termination of an agreement to trade goods/services, on death, bankruptcy, insolvency or winding up).
Investor Shares / Accounts Created when surpluses are allocated or financial capital is contributed.	When Labour/User shareholders invest capital and/or when capital gains are allocated to them.	At the end of each year when the enterprise is valued (and sets a new 'fair price', if a company).	Settled on retirement or death, unless they have been transferred (or earmarked for transfer) to a mutual for employee, community or public benefit.

- Founder Shares / Memberships are linked to a stewardship role, to ensure the socio-economic goals of the founders influence decision-making:

- Labour Shares / Membership are linked to a continuous working role in (or for) the organisation, creating and trading the products and services on which the organisation depends. Labour shareholders derive income from their Labour Shares;

- User Shares / Membership are linked to a customer / service user role, continually using or buying the products and

---

[96] FairShares Model Company Rules, clauses 10(a) (i-iv). Clause numbering is the same across company, cooperative and association model rules.

services offered by the organisation. User shareholders derive income from their User Shares.

- Investor Shares / Accounts represent the financial interest that investors, the workforce and customers develop as the enterprise increases its capacity to generate wealth. Investor shares represent members' interest in the wealth they have created, but which has not been distributed to them. Dividends or Interest are paid on Investor Shares, but not on Investor Accounts. Investor Accounts hold money that members can allocate to projects of their choice.

Figure 1.5 – Share characteristics[97]

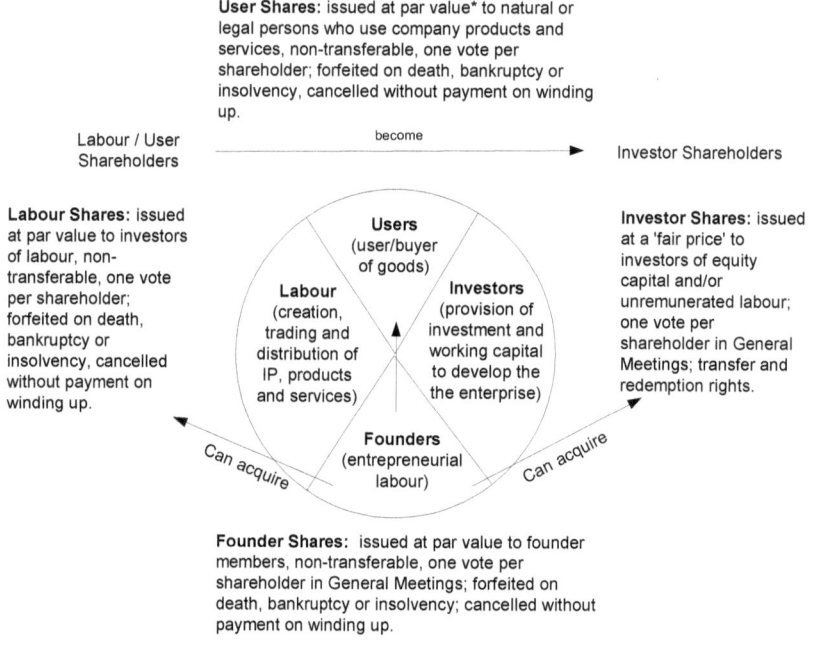

Copyright 2013, Rory Ridley-Duff, Cliff Southcombe and Nicci Dickins
Creative Commons 4.0 Licence, BY-NC-SA

---

[97] *ibid.*, clause 10(a)

By default, all voting is on a one-person, one-vote basis irrespective of the number of shares held, or the number of shareholder / membership groups to which a person belongs.[98] However, when a special resolution is required, a person's vote will count in each shareholder / membership group they belong to because a special resolution requires majority support from each *group* to pass.

These ownership and governance arrangements promote the socialisation, rather than the privatisation, of power and wealth.

To create an intellectual commons, members allow commercialisation of their IP:[99]

- when a person creates IP, they may choose to license it to a FairShares Enterprise (whether he/she is a member or not); but
- if the IP was produced by a member as part of a labour or supply contract paid for by the Enterprise, then the IP creator must license it to the Enterprise (this can be enshrined in employment or service contracts); the Enterprise has an exclusive right to commercialize the IP for the duration of the IP creators' period of membership.
- after an IP creator leaves an Enterprise, the Enterprise retains a non-exclusive right to commercialize all of the IP which the creator previously licensed to the Enterprise.
- after an IP creator leaves an Enterprise, the creator retains a non-exclusive right to all of the IP they have previously created, including IP which was produced as part of a labour or supply contract and paid for by the Enterprise.

These IP arrangements promote the socialisation, rather than the privatisation, of intellectual property. Just as a financial investor gets back both their original capital plus a dividend, so an intellectual (labour) investor gets back both their

---

[98] *ibid.*, clauses 21 to 24.
[99] *ibid.*, clause 53.

original capital plus any dividend to which they are entitled.[100]

Some limitations

Under these rules, it may be harder (in the short term) to secure grants from charitable or public sources, or from investors who do not wish to support democratic (one-person, one vote) cooperative governance. They are suitable for employee and/or community ownership where social entrepreneurs want to spread wealth and power and harness the power of a membership model in raising financial, intellectual and social capital. As Investor Shares can be traded with mutual institutions defined in the Articles of Association, investors can design an exit route from the outset.

How does a FairShares enterprise evolve?

The development model below is based on PhD research in 2004/5[101] to reflect *what actually happens* in successful companies that transfer from private to mutual ownership. The framework helps to understand how an enterprise can evolve from a (single person) start-up venture to a fully developed FairShares cooperative, company or association.[102] By combining mutual ownership and cooperative governance to achieve long term sustainability.

---

[100] McCulloch and Ridley-Duff, 'Beyond Accounting for Capitals'.
[101] Ridley-Duff, 'Communitarian Perspectives on Corporate Governance', http://shura.shu.ac.uk/2681/.
[102] The example provided is based on Company Law. However, many of the principles apply to Co-operative Law as well. In the Co-operative Law version of the FairShares Model, Investor Shares have a par value. The Articles of Association for a FairShares Co-operative include provision for a Redemption Fund that enables users to redeem their Investor Shares in a way that does not put the enterprise at risk. In an Association, Investor Accounts hold any money allocated to a

Importantly, the direction of travel is more important than the starting point. It helps to remember that it is not necessary to create all institutions at the outset (indeed, it might be overwhelming and/or compromise the survival of the enterprise). So long as the pathway is understood, and the institutions needed are known in advance, they can gradually be created when there is time and resources to do so. The pages that follow provide a guide to the way sustainable mutual enterprises have developed.

This model assumes that entrepreneurs will be more attracted to the *FairShares Model* if both social and financial rewards are available, and that they will be able to realise a 'fair share' of the value their entrepreneurial efforts create. In doing so, a social rather than private enterprise pathway is outlined, in which value is carefully shared rather than privately accumulated, culminating in the mutualisation of private shareholdings.[103] An exit route characterised by a gradual conversion to mutual ownership replaces the conventional exit route of a public floatation or private sale.

After the efforts of the founders to establish a profitable enterprise bear fruit, the model outlines the establishment (and use) of mutual organisations to buy Investors Shares from founders, producers and customers (users). This provides them with equitable returns for past efforts without privatising the wealth they have created.

Development takes place in three phases:

- Phase 1 – Informal Democracy
- Phase 2 – Embryonic Democratic Model
- Phase 3 – Social Democracy / Cooperative Governance

---

member. It is held in trust until they reinvest it in projects of their choosing - it cannot be withdrawn.

[103] Model Company Rules, clause 10(a) (iv) (1).

Phase 1 – Informal democracy

During this phase, social entrepreneur(s) (or a group of founding members) establish an enterprise using their own financial resources and/or easily accessible grant/loan finance (Figure 1.6).

a) *Established by*: founder members/social entrepreneur(s)

b) *Share Allocation*: all founders receive one Founder Share / Membership. All founders working in the enterprise receive Labour Shares / Membership in proportion to their labour. In a company or cooperative, founders can contribute risk capital as Investor Shares, or receive a proportion of their income as Investor Shares to make a capital contribution.

c) *Characterised by:* entrepreneurial group with informal consultation and feedback mechanisms. General Meetings and dialogue between all staff with no discrete governing body.

d) *Ends when:* it is no longer possible to run the company effectively through a combination of interactive communications and General Meetings. The pressure to move to Phase 2 will being to grow when the number of members exceed 8, particularly when both Labour and User Shares / Memberships have been issued to new members.

e) *Shared Prosperity*:[104] through qualifying contributions new employees receive Labour Shares. After trading commences, User Shares are issued for qualifying contributions. By default, labour and user shareholders (members) receive 70% of the surplus (35% to each group).[105] The remaining 30% is controlled by Investor Shareholders / Account Holders.[106] In a FairShares cooperative / company, half the 'capital gain' is allocated each year as Investor Shares to the holders of Labour and User Shares (so Labour and User Shareholder eventually acquire Investor Shares even if they cannot afford to buy them

---

[104] *ibid.*, clauses 10, 12 and 15.
[105] *ibid.*, clause 40.
[106] *ibid.*, clause 44.

directly).[107] This broadens the ownership of Investor Shares and remains 'fair' by allocating them to Labour and User Shareholders in proportion to their qualifying contributions.

f) *Funded By*: founders subscribing capital, grants, debt finance.

Figure 1.6 – Early stage shareholdings / membership

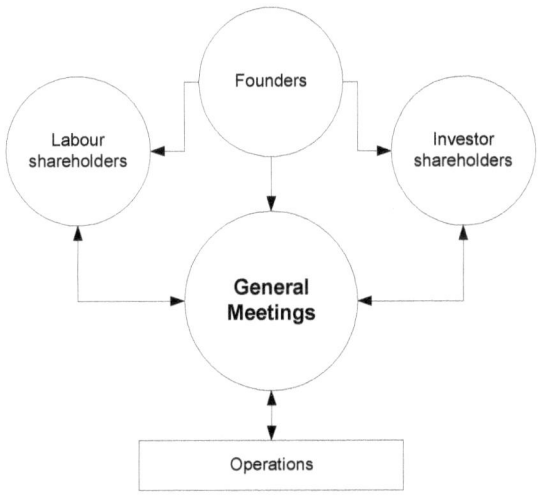

Copyright 2013, Rory Ridley-Duff
Creative Commons 4.0 Licence, BY-NC-SA

---

[107] *ibid.*, clause 15(a) and (b).

Phase 2 – Embryonic democratic model

In this phase, new employees (and regular suppliers) acquire more Labour and Investor Shares. Users acquire more Investor Shares (Figure 1.7). More involvement and participation in governance is practised. The enterprise experiments with democratic governance models and practices, but founder-led / manager-led consultations are likely to remain dominant in policy development / strategic management. Separate processes develop as people begin to specialise in governance, management and operations. Social auditing arrangements are put in place.

a) *Established by*: founders, second generation of employees / producers, first / second generation of users.
b) *Characterised by:* development of work teams and embryonic governing bodies for Founder, Labour and User Shareholders, and investors. General Meetings involve new Labour and User Shareholders.
c) *Ends when:* financial and growth thresholds are met (typically somewhere between 20 and 50 members, set in Articles of Association).[108]
d) *Shared Prosperity*: Number of Labour and User Shareholders increase. More Labour and User Shareholders begin to acquire Investor Shares.[109] Opportunities to buy Investor Shares increase. Work

---

[108] *ibid.*, clause 29, 30 and 47. On reaching a threshold set in the rules, members start electing directors, implementing multi-stakeholder governance and elect an audit committee.

[109] *ibid.*, clause 12 defines the right of Labour and User shareholders to buy Investor shares after 1 year. Clause 15 defines the issue of Member shares to Labour and User Shareholders when surpluses are generated.

begins on institutions to redeem (and trade) Investor Shares amongst members and mutual institutions.[110]

a) *Funded By*: capital from new and existing members; debt finance.

Figure 1.7 – Evolution of shareholdings

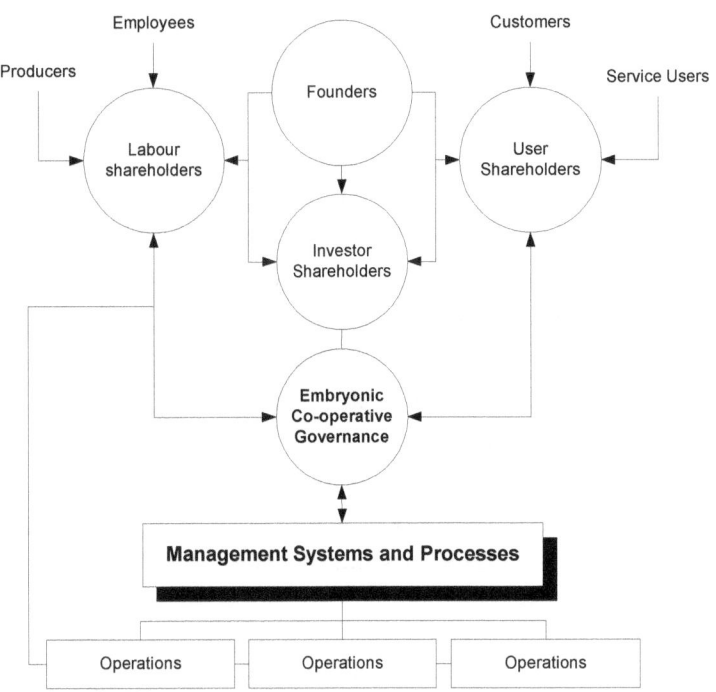

Copyright 2013, Rory Ridley-Duff
Creative Commons 4.0 Licence, BY-NC-SA

---

[110] Model Company Rules, clause 10(iv) defines the institutions.

Phase 3 – Social democracy / cooperative governance

In this phase, democratic structures are established (Figure 1.8), ownership and surplus sharing arrangements are formalised, and wealth and assets are locked into the community under the philosophy of 'distributism'.[111] Mutual organisations are created to manage social wealth.[112]

a) *Established by*: reaching the size threshold set at incorporation in the Articles of Association.

b) Characterised by:
   - elections to governing bodies drawn from the pool of Founder, Labour, User and Investor Shareholders (members)
   - the creation of forums for debate by (and between) Founder, Labour, User and Investor Shareholders
   - refined administrative systems to allocate Labour Shares to new employees (and producers)
   - refined administrative systems to allocate User Shares to established customers/services users
   - refined administrative systems to allocate Investor Shares to suppliers, customers and service users with long-term relationships;
   - defined management systems to organise new issues of Investor Shares to raise risk capital;
   - defined mutual funds / organisations for employee, community and public benefit start operating.

c) *Shared Prosperity:* through the ongoing issue of Labour and User Shares to new members so that they acquire Investor Shares; through increasing the number of Investor Shares transferred into mutual ownership for employee, community and public benefit.

---

[111] Boyd, 'Chesterton and Distributism'.
[112] Model Company Rules, clauses 11(a), 16(c).

d) *Funded By:* issues of Investor Shares, members' capital contributions, loan finance (if needed).

e) *Secured By:* mutualisation of investor shareholdings as members leave, retire or become insolvent/bankrupt.

Figure 1.8 – Finalisation of institutions

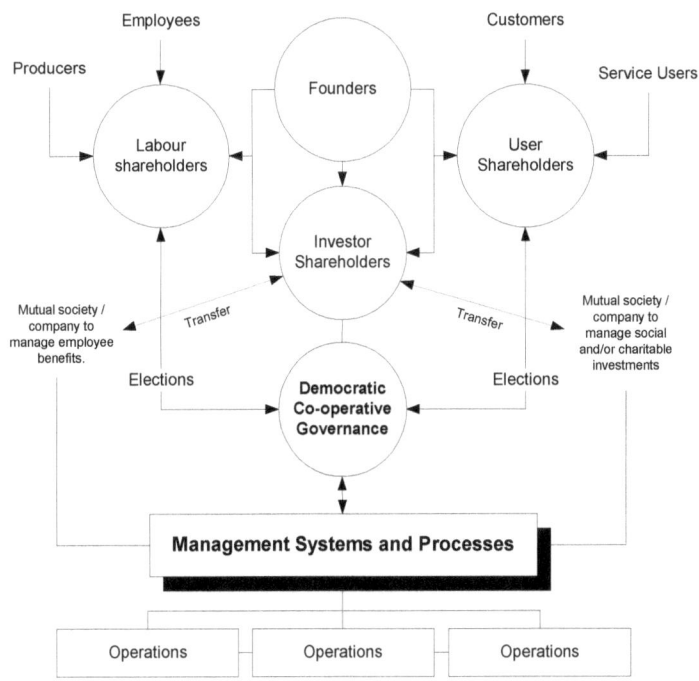

Copyright 2013, Rory Ridley-Duff
Creative Commons 4.0 Licence, BY-NC-SA

How do shareholders access wealth?

A system for members to recover capital they have invested (both directly and indirectly) and receive a share of any additional value that has accrued as a result of enterprise development combines the cooperative and private sector systems of entrepreneurial reward. Past mutual models have been premised on the assumption that members will not necessarily want to recover their capital. This argument weakens over time as members sustain their efforts to create wealth and sometimes need to realise it to survive personal and family crises.[113]

As labour investments increase, so the concept of 'fair shares' becomes more important. The idea that new members should gradually build up their entitlement to a share of rewards is a product of experience in both worker and consumer cooperatives.[114] The idea that residual value (the unallocated wealth created by the efforts of all members past and present) can be distributed to members or passed to / shared with charitable institutions is well established in cooperative economics.

In the last 50 years, the increasing use of employee benefit trusts, charitable trusts and various mutual enterprises to purchase / redeem members' shares has largely solved the puzzle of how to sustain an entrepreneurial culture in employee-owned and mutual enterprises over long periods of time.[115] Various approaches have been recommended: redemption after a fixed period (5 – 10 years), share purchases upon leaving or retiring, allocations of shares to trusts.[116] For this purpose, 50% of reserves are held as a Redemption Fund to pay for the creation of mutual organisations and transfers of shares.[117] By default, a FairShares Enterprise has about 5 years to work on the creation of the mutual institutions that will redeem members' shareholdings (as this is likely to be the minimum period before transfer rights can be exercised).

David Ellerman makes a powerful case for protecting democracy at work by arguing that a member's right to vote and share residual assets should not outlive them (i.e.

---

[113] Ridley-Duff, 'Cooperative social enterprises'.
[114] Ellerman, 'The Democratic Firm'.
[115] Rodrick, 'Leveraged ESOPs and Employee Buyouts'; Erdal, 'Beyond the Corporation'.
[116] McDonnell, MacKnight and Donnelly, 'Democratic Enterprise'.
[117] FairShares Model Company Rules, clause 37.

should not be inheritable).[118] To achieve this, the transfer of voting and residual asset rights to a mutual society/company takes place when a member leaves, retires, dies or becomes insolvent. Members who transfer their shares into mutual ownership can become members of the cooperative, company or association to which they are transferred. This enables them to continue exercising their voice in decisions on how their legacy is invested for member, community and public benefit. If an individual member dies or organisational member winds up, their Investor shares are redeemed or transferred. Any proceeds go into their estate.[119]

How can these ideas be applied to practice?

Application in worker-owned enterprises

In a worker cooperative the emphasis is on issuing Labour Shares to those contributing labour (employees and suppliers with open-ended supply contracts), then allocating profits as Investor Shares in proportion to labour shareholdings annually. By default, 35% of surpluses are distributed to Labour shareholders. As Labour Shares are issued at a nominal cost of £1 / €1 / $1, there is no barrier to becoming a labour shareholder. Those contributing more labour receive larger rewards. Many successful co-owned businesses use a similar incentive system whereby share distributions based on annual profitability contribute to an entrepreneurial culture with a highly committed workforce (St Luke's Advertising Agency and School Trends offer two examples).

No up-front contributions are necessary as the investor shareholdings are generated as a by-product of creating a

---

[118] Model Company Rules, clause 10(v), from Ellerman, 'The Democratic Firm'.
[119] Model Company Rules, clause 10. Cooperative, clauses 10 and 11.

profitable trading enterprise.[120] However, capital contributions help reduce the cost of capital for investment. Staff can increase their investor shareholdings by buying additional shares, or can be required to buy shares upon joining. At School Trends Ltd, for example, staff must buy a shareholding equal to 5% of their starting salary after one year of service (with a cap set at 5% of share capital). At Gripple, staff buy £1000 of shares upon joining (funded by a loan if necessary).[121] In the Mondragon Cooperative Corporation, a person makes a capital contribution equal to two months' salary, funded by reserves or a bank loan if necessary.[122]

In FairShares Model Articles of Association (see Part 3), founders and members may decide not to define a qualifying contribution for User Shares. In this case, the rules provide for branding the enterprise as a Labour Association, Worker Cooperative or Employee-Owned Enterprise.[123]

Application in user-owned enterprises

In a user cooperative, the key goal is to benefit the people who trade or use the enterprise's products/services.[124] It is particularly appropriate for cooperative ventures where there is 'production for use' rather than 'production for market' (such as tenant-owned/run housing, food cooperatives and educational projects). User Shares are issued when a user is accepted as a member (usually after

---

[120] Ridley-Duff, 'Cooperative social enterprises'.
[121] Information sourced from the Employee Ownership Association during the writing of Ridley-Duff, 'Communitarian governance in social enterprises'. A new study by David Wren at Sheffield Business School is due for completion in late 2015.
[122] Recently reconfirmed by Bird, 'Co-operation and Business Services'.
[123] FairShares Model Rules, clause 10 (all variants).
[124] Parnell, 'Co-operation: The Beautiful Idea'.

trading/using the organisation's products or services for a fixed period of time).[125] Investor Shares are issued when the enterprise generates profits or when members subscribe capital. Dividends are paid to user shareholders based on the value of products/services they have traded.

In some cases, labour and user shareholders may not be totally distinct groups (for example, members of a housing cooperative, food cooperative, community shop / pub may contribute labour to run them while also buying goods/services). In these cases, a judgement is needed about the effect of issuing both User and Labour shares.

In FairShares Model Articles of Association (see Part 3), founders and members may decide not to define a qualifying contribution for Labour Shares. In this case, the rules provide for branding the enterprise as a User Association, User Cooperative or User-Owned Enterprise.[126]

Application in a cooperative consortium

In a cooperative consortium, Founder Shares can be issued to individuals or organisations who establish the consortium. Labour Shares can be issued to members in proportion to the amount of labour they supply, User Shares can be issued to members who contract to purchase goods and services, and Investor Shares can be issued to members in proportion to the capital contributions they make. This way, dividends are paid to members for labour, user and capital investments. The collective interests of the founders are protected through the voice reserved for Founder Shares in decision-making and governance.[127]

The workforce can participate by acquiring Labour and Investor Shares in their own right following the mechanisms

---

[125] FairShares Model Company/Cooperative Rules, clause 12.
[126] *ibid.*, clause 10 (all variants).
[127] *ibid.*, clauses 29-31.

for allocating Labour Shares decided in General Meeting. By way of example, they might be allocated as follows: 10 shares per FTE equivalent member of staff (this allows for fractional work – 1 share = 0.5 days a week, 2 shares = 1 day a week etc.); one share per 100 hours of (volunteer) labour provided; one share per £10k of labour provided. Any equitable system agreed by members is valid.

The criteria for issuing Labour and User shares is defined by the qualifying contribution set by members in General Meeting. Anyone who makes a qualifying contribution is entitled to apply for membership.

How to convert to a FairShares association

Of all the possible conversions, on paper this is the most straightforward. In practice, it may be the most complicated. In theory, an association can adopt a new constitution (see Part 3, Model Rules for a FairShares Association) by following the procedures set out in its existing constitution. In practice, there may be clauses in funding contracts, loan agreements on top of statutory regulation restricting changes to specific clauses (like 'objects'), or even the entire constitution. This applies particularly if operating as a charity or statutory association. It means that a lengthy set of negotiations may be needed with any party into which a binding contract has been entered.

There is, therefore, no sensible general advice that can be given about conversion to an association without first acquiring a detailed understanding of the contracts, funding agreements and regulation that governs the association's work. What I can say, however, is that the more an association generates its own income, the more freedom it is likely to have to change its constitution.

If you get as far as agreeing you can amend the constitution, it is worth considering the value of appointing existing Trustees as the (new) association's Founder

Members. Service users who meet an agreed 'qualifying contribution' can become its User members. There is one caveat, however. If your existing constitution requires rotation of elected Trustee Board members, it may be better to avoid appointing Founder Members altogether (so that elections and rotations can continue). The newly formed association can debate and decide on the merits of extending membership to employees and volunteers (subject to any statutory or local laws that place restrictions on this).

Starting a FairShares Association is much more straightforward. If not incorporating:

1. assemble founders;
2. agree how to adapt the Model Rules for a FairShares Association;
3. agree and set your objects (clause 5);
4. call a meeting of the Founders to pass a resolution to adopt the new constitution you have agreed.

You are now up and running as a FairShares Association (and you can brand yourself as a Solidarity, Labour or User Association depend on the qualifying contributions you set for members).[128]

If incorporating, you will have to review and satisfy the regulatory requirements that apply in your country/region (e.g. the requirements for registering as a charity, association or Company Limited by Guarantee). Even if you do incorporate, the first step is likely to be the same (agree a FairShares constitution). For a new association, it may be better to stick to only Founder Members until you have met regulatory requirements. It is much easier to amend your rules when the number of members is small. It may also help to hire a professional who can guide you through the regulations, but do not take advice about FairShares itself

---

[128] *ibid.*, clause 10.

from anyone unless you are satisfied that they have received appropriate training or have professional experience of establishing solidarity enterprises (you can use the FairShares Online Community to find someone if you have any doubts). Many supporters of the FairShares Association are consultants and will be in a good position to help you.

How to convert to a FairShares company

Converting to a company – because it is more likely to generate its own funding and be free of restrictions on changes to its rules - is likely to be more straightforward. It will be easiest, ironically, if the shares already issued are in the hands of a single person or small group of people. The more people holding shares, the harder you will have to work to convince them of the value of changing to a FairShares constitution. There is, however, a clear pathway for converting a private company in most cases.

1. Identify whether there is a dominant interest group (a person, organisation or group of investors who hold a majority of shares and exercise ultimate control).
2. Adapt the Model Rules for a FairShares Company to issue a Founder share to each party who is part of the dominant interest group.
3. Ask the Founders to add 'objects' that are important to them (Clause 5) and register a new company. [129]
4. If you want to carry on with the same Board of Directors, convene a General Meeting and use the powers conferred on the Founders to appoint the Board members.
5. Use the valuation process set out in Clause 13 to calculate the value of the existing private company (including the 'Fair

---

[129] In the UK, use the IN01 form and remember to tick 'Bespoke Rules' so you can attach your constitution when you submit your application to register.

Price' at which shares will start to trade). To do this, use the *filed* accounts for the previous accounting period.

6. Organise a transfer of undertaking (TUPE) to formally transfer contracts, assets and staff from the old legal entity to the new one.
7. Issue Investor Shares to all existing ordinary shareholders at the Fair Price in proportion to their existing ordinary shareholdings.
8. Agree the 'qualifying contribution' for Labour shares and issue Labour shares to existing employees, suppliers and contractors who meet the qualifying contribution (they won't earn anything, or acquire any Investor Shares, until the new legal entity generates a surplus). They will, however, start to acquire a voice in company governance.
9. Agree the 'qualifying contribution' for User shares and issue User shares to existing customers, users or beneficiaries who meet the qualifying contribution (they too won't earn anything, or acquire any Investor Shares, until the new legal entity generates a surplus).
10. At the end of the *following* accounting period (at least 1 year after the transfer of undertaking), Labour and User shareholders will be entitled to purchase Investor Shares at the Fair Price operating at that time.
11. Following Clause 15 ('Members Shares'), existing shareholders can now transfer ownership of their Investor shares to Labour and User Shareholders (and receive compensation at the Fair Price).
12. Following Clauses 10 and 12, existing shareholders can also create trusts, charities, (FairShares) associations, (FairShares) cooperatives and (FairShares) companies that manage shareholdings for member, community and public benefit. Investor shareholders can sell their shareholdings these mutual organisations (and also join them to continue

exercising a voice over how the income from their shareholdings are allocated).[130]

13. Over time, Investor Shareholdings will be acquired by Labour and User Shareholders without compromising co-operative values and principles.

A similar process could be followed for the conversion of an existing cooperative (or private company) to a FairShares Cooperative. However, as cooperatives are member-led (rather than investor-led) enterprises you may be faced with a different enterprise culture. Existing co-operatives may be member-controlled (with no shares), or member-owned (with shares). The following section provides you with an approach to converting both types of cooperative.

Converting member-*controlled* cooperatives

In the UK, member-controlled co-operatives can be established as a Company Limited by Guarantee without share capital. In these cases, there are often propriety mechanisms for distributing surpluses. If these mechanisms work well, it may be better to adapt the Model Rules for a FairShares Association (removing any restrictions in the rules on paying dividends to members, and incorporating under a Companies Act). This will help promote continuity with existing arrangements.

In all cases, make the old cooperative the Founder Member of the new cooperative association. By doing so, whatever decision-making mechanisms exist already can continue to operate in the new cooperative. If the existing cooperative is a worker cooperative, members will now become Labour members in the FairShares cooperative. If the existing cooperative is a consumer cooperative, existing

---

[130] The professional skills / knowledge of employee-ownership experts will be particularly helpful in this period because they are likely to be familiar with creating employee and/or charitable trusts.

members will now become User members. As cooperatives must establish criteria for membership, these criteria become the 'qualifying contribution' for existing and new members. After re-constituting, the new cooperative members can debate whether to extend the qualifying contribution to both Labour and User members or retain the status quo.

Converting member-*owned* cooperatives

In many countries there are laws for registering cooperatives that can issue equity. These are member-*owned* cooperatives (because members will have par value cooperative shares). Initially, see if you can follow the provisions in the existing constitution (and Cooperative Laws) to adopt new rules. If you can, then you can design and adopt a new constitution within your existing rules. If not, establish a new FairShares cooperative in which the old cooperative is the Founder Member. As detailed above, this permits members of the old cooperative to make decisions about the new cooperative using its existing approach to decision-making before it admits additional members.

As with associations, you may need to check with funders and statutory authorities that they are happy for you to transfer contracts and assets to the new legal form. They may require changes to your FairShares cooperative rules before they approve any transfer of undertaking.

The process then unfolds roughly as follows:

1. Convert all existing members' capital to par value Investor Shares in the new FairShares cooperative.
2. Make existing criteria for membership the new 'qualifying contribution' for membership and issue Labour / User shares to all existing members who satisfy the qualifying contribution (this gives them their voice in governance).
3. At the end of the *following* accounting period (at least 1 year after the transfer of undertaking), Labour and User members will be entitled to purchase additional Investor Shares if they wish.

The Need for Change

4. Following Clause 15 ('Members Shares'), existing Labour / User shareholders will start to receive additional Investor shares whenever there are good trading results.
5. Following Clause 11 ('Withdrawals'), members can withdraw their Investor Shares (subject to the funds in the Redemption Fund).
6. Following Clauses 10, 12 and 16, existing members can create trusts, charities, (FairShares) associations, (FairShares) cooperatives and (FairShares) companies to manage shareholdings for the benefit of members, community or the public.
7. Over time, Investor Shareholdings will grow and shrink as capital is created and lost from the enterprise. This will occur without a loss of control by members, and without compromising co-operative values and principles.

In practice, this may mean that voting power that used to be integrated into a single membership type is now split between Investor membership (for the management of members' financial capital holdings) and Labour/User membership (for the management of their voice and dividend rights).

How to convert between legal forms

At this point in time, the process from changing from one type of legal structures to another has not been considered in any detail and we recommend professional advice combined with advice from the FairShares Online Community. As knowledge of practice develops, information about the process it will appear in new editions of this book.

Where (exactly) did these ideas come from?

The *FairShares Model* owes a debt to studies of Yugoslav[131] labour-managed firms by Jaroslav Vanek,[132] and subsequent works by David Ellerman,[133] Shann Turnbull[134] and David Erdal.[135] Most draw on successful models of worker and employee-ownership, particularly cooperatives in the Basque region around Mondragon in Spain.[136] The immediate antecedent, however, is the work of Guy Major and Gavin Body on a 'Democratic Business' model.[137] This was developed further by me at Computercraft Ltd, First Contact Software Ltd, New Horizons Music Ltd, Social Exchange Ltd, before becoming embedded in teaching materials, research and knowledge transfer work undertaken at Sheffield Business School.[138]

Major and Boby's model rules were promoted to cooperative and private businesses in the period 1999 - 2002.[139] I developed their ideas through joint work with

---

[131] After the Yugoslav wars, Yugoslavia divided in the following states: Croatia, Slovenia, Macedonia, Bosnia and Herzegovina and the Federal Republic of Yugoslavia (Serbia). In 2006, Montenegro separated from Serbia.
[132] Vanek, 'The General Theory of Labor-Managed Market Economies'
[133] Ellerman, 'Entrepreneurship in the Mondragon Co-operatives', 'The Democratic Worker-Owned Firm', 'Helping People Help Themselves'.
[134] Turnbull, 'Stakeholder democracy', 'Innovations in corporate governance', 'A New Way to Govern'.
[135] Erdal, 'The Psychology of Sharing', 'Local Heroes', 'Beyond the Corporation'.
[136] See Whyte and Whyte, 'Making Mondragon', Ridley-Duff, 'Communitarian governance in social enterprises'.
[137] Major, 'Solving the under-investment and degeneration problems of worker co-ops', 'The Need for NOVARs', Major and Boby, 'Equity Devaluation'.
[138] Ridley-Duff and Bull, 'Understanding Social Enterprise'.
[139] As reflected in *Silent Revolution*, my first attempt at a publication about social enterprise management published in 2002.

Peter Beeby and Rick Norris (School Trends Ltd) during a PhD study.[140] The idea of combining internal (direct) membership with external collective ownership (including trust-based ownership) is derived from discussion documents at the Employee Share Ownership Center in the US and Employee Ownership Association in the UK. This attempts to re-create in UK / US Company Law arrangements similar to the successful Mondragon Cooperative Corporation (MCC).[141]

My PhD advanced *communitarian pluralism* and a 'surplus sharing' iteration of Major and Boby's democratic business model.[142] This was checked by a professor of Corporate Law at Sheffield Hallam University in light of the (then) forthcoming Companies Act 2006. The model was revised again in January, October and December 2009 to reflect further changes in UK Company Law. In 2010, clarifications of the way rules can be used to support the development of 'solidarity cooperatives' and 'cooperative consortia' were made. Minor changes were made in March 2010 following discussions with Connie Thorpe and Morgan Killick (a Business Link social enterprise advisor and award winning social entrepreneur in the Yorkshire and Humber region of the UK). These changes focused on making model rules more attractive to social investors.

---

[140] This is clearer in a joint submission to the government consultation on Community Interest Companies in 2003. Aside from Ridley-Duff's actual PhD, further papers based on it were published including: 'Communitarian perspectives on social enterprise', 'Social enterprise as a socially rational business' and 'Communitarian governance in social enterprises'.

[141] Brown, 'Design equity finance for social enterprises', Erdal, 'Beyond the Corporation'.

[142] SHU, 'Democratising Cooperatives, Charities and Social Enterprises', http://impact.ref.ac.uk/CaseStudies/CaseStudy.aspx?Id=4965; See Ridley-Duff and Bull, 'Understanding Social Enterprise' Case 7.4.

Other important influences include the NewCo Model prepared by Bill Barker and Morgan Killick at the Sheffield Community Economic Development Unit,[143] and particularly the developments at ESP Projects Ltd that combined shares with cooperative and private sector characteristics to satisfy different constituencies. The Stakeholder Model prepared by Geof Cox for the Common Cause Foundation,[144] and the Somerset Rules[145] prepared by Somerset Co-operative Services have also influenced teaching and debate amongst post-graduate students of cooperative and social enterprise at Sheffield Business School.[146] Each of these models – developed independently – influenced the FairShares Model by embracing multi-stakeholder democratic principles.[147] They confirm a broad interest in the concept of a solidarity enterprise that binds together the interests of different stakeholders to create a social economy.[148]

The final pieces of this puzzle were put in place after discussions about intellectual property and worker alienation at the School for Democratic Socialism (held between September 2011 and May 2012 in Sheffield). This influenced collaborative work between myself at Sheffield Business School and Cliff Southcombe at Social Enterprise

---

[143] Killick and Ridley-Duff, in Ridley-Duff and Bull, 'Understanding Social Enterprise' Case 7.3.

[144] Cox and Ridley-Duff in, Ridley-Duff and Bull, 'Understanding Social Enterprise' Case 7.1

[145] For the latest versions see: http://www.somerset.coop/p/somerset-rules-registrations.html, accessed 24th May 2015.

[146] Ridley-Duff and Southcombe, 'The Social Enterprise Mark'. Winner of 'Best Paper' award at the 31st ISBE Conference for its critique of the Social Enterprise Mark and use in knowledge transfer work.

[147] Brown, 'Designing equity finance for social enterprises', Lund, 'Solidarity as a Business Model'.

[148] McDonnell, MacKnight and Donnelly, 'Democratic Enterprise', Atherton et al., 'Practical Tools for Defining Co-operative and Mutual Enterprises', Birchall, 'A member-owned business approach to the classification of co-operatives and mutuals'.

Europe Ltd. At the School for Democratic Socialism, the success of Wikipedia was debated. I wrote discussion paper on Creative Commons licensing to circulate amongst the school participants, the Co-operative Group and local Co-operative Party.[149] This paper proposed Wikipedia's approach to Intellectual Property (IP) become the basis of a bond amongst cooperative members. The creators of IP license it to their enterprise using Creative Commons Licences, but do not transfer ownership.[150] Individuals and groups, therefore, share IP with other workforce members without becoming alienated from the IP they create. If worker members grant exclusive commercial rights to the association, cooperative or social enterprise they work for (and non-exclusive rights if they leave or work part-time), a fuller expression of cooperative and social enterprise values and principles becomes possible. Importantly, it ends the alienation that occurs when members of the workforce cannot control the 'fruits of their labour'.

The papers and discussion documents prepared by Ridley-Duff and Southcombe[151] helped to embed this 'socialisation' perspective in the delivery of Cooperative and Social Enterprise Schools at Sheffield Business School (co-delivered with Social Enterprise Yorkshire & Humber, Social Enterprise Europe and Co-operative Business Consultants). Since 2013, the FairShares Association has been practising how to put 'socialisation' into practice to build the IP on which FairShares is based.

Co-operative and Social Enterprise Support Ltd (a company) and the FairShares Association (an association) have been created to take forward this collaboration and test out model rules. The FairShares Model is ripe for promotion

---

[149] Ridley-Duff, 'Creative Commons'.
[150] Model Rules, clause 53.
[151] Ridley-Duff and Southcombe, 'The Social Enterprise Mark'.

to educational institutions, cooperatives, mutuals, social enterprises, consultants and (social) entrepreneurs. That is where the supporters and members of the FairShares Association will take a lead.

Conclusions

In Part 1 of this book, an integrated argument has been made to support 'The Case for FairShares'. Initially, I argued that changes in the cooperative movement led to a rediscovery of the value of worker ownership.[152] Pursued through worker cooperatives, employee-owned businesses and (more recently) solidarity enterprises with worker and consumer owners, a vibrant and resilient form of new cooperativism is spreading throughout Spain, France, Italy, Scandinavia, Canada, the USA and UK as well as parts of Eastern Europe, Africa, South America and Asia.[153] A 'multi-stakeholder turn' has been reinforced by global arguments for sustainable development and calls from the United Nations for 'responsible management education'.[154] Hundreds of business schools have taken up the challenge.

Actors in the public, private and third sectors are now busy converging on an enterprise model that is inclusive, cooperative, oriented towards shared value creation – a 'for purpose' **fourth sector**. The enterprise models of the fourth sector need coherent theories and compelling articulations of their underlying principles and practices that will meet the aspirations of a new generation of social entrepreneurs.

In the second half of Part 1, I examined how these aspirations came together in the publication of the *FairShares Model*. I carefully examined how FairShares frames core concepts, embraces pluralism and takes a new approach to

---

[152] Novkovic and Webb, 'Co-operatives in a Post-Growth Era'.
[153] Roelants et al., 'Co-operatives and Employment'.
[154] Laasch and Conway, 'Principles of Responsible Management'.

ownership and governance. I suggested that it is infused with the spirit of 'new co-operativism', committed to 'open cooperation' (using Creative Commons) and has internalised 'solidarity as a business model'. Towards the end of Part 1, I set out findings on how robust mutual enterprises (including FairShares enterprises) can develop over time. This involved linking the arguments in the text to the Articles of Association in Part 3.

In Part 2 of this book, I take up a different challenge. I set out educational materials, social auditing techniques and management diagnostics that have developed to support the teaching of FairShares values and principles. This is a key task. Reshaping thoughts, building confidence in new ideas (perhaps in the face of scepticism or opposition) takes intellectual energy, time and experimentation. Without an educational strategy (including a vibrant debate about curricula), people energised by these ideas will fall back on practices familiar to them whenever they feel stuck (whether the familiar practices work or not!). The educational activities in Part 2 will help you (and others) to find your pathway into FairShares and evaluate your own progress. They will help you distinguish which ideas are supportive and destructive to FairShares.

This is particularly true in the area of Intellectual Property management. We are imbued with the idea of whoever *pays* for our work is automatically entitled to the ideas that we generate (usually within an employment relationship or contract for services). We are uniquely unprepared for the earthquake that arises when this assumption starts to change. But change it must if FairShares is to succeed. Switching to the assumption that whoever *develops* an idea has an inalienable right to be its co-owner (regardless of the contract under it was developed or how it was paid for) will be the biggest challenge in taking the *FairShares Model* forward. It goes to the heart of a debate about who is entitled to own the ideas that are used to build our systems of production. It challenges the basis of capitalism - that the owner of financial capital invested in people and machinery is entitled to own the products of their labour. FairShares offers a different vision. The people who create IP are *always* entitled to (cooperatively) shape how the wealth their ideas generate will be allocated, together with the people who pay for its creation.

The activities described in Part 2, and the online tools developed to support them, will help stimulate debate about these issues. They have been built incrementally since 2008 at Sheffield Business School. They include questions that need to be asked for people to discover how to make FairShares work in different contexts. They have been used on MSc teaching programmes (Co-operative and Social Enterprise Management / Charity Resource Management / International Human Resource Management). New educational ideas keep developing (e.g. *The Dragons' Apprentice: a social enterprise novel*).

With each passing year, the character and quality of the activities and materials will develop. By publishing them in this volume, I hope a new community will spring up that embraces the challenge of developing FairShares education. I look forward to learning from you how you are using, embedding and developing them. I will join you in that endeavour by continuing to embed FairShares where it is appropriate to do so in cooperative business, social enterprise and responsible management courses. I will also continue to research the impact of FairShares on workplace democracy.

So, in finalising Part 1, I invite you to leave the world of academic study and enter the world of engaged practice. Join me in discovering how to engage groups of people in learning about FairShares, to ramp up the level of debate and discussion, to take ideas from the page into the classroom, around the dinner table, and – eventually – into the Board Room.

References

Alvord, S., Brown, D. and Letts, C. (2004) 'Social entrepreneurship and societal transformation: an exploratory study', *Journal of Applied Behavioural Science,* 40: 260-282.

Atherton, J., Birchall, J., Mayo, E. and Simon, G. (2012) *Practical Tools for Defining Co-operative and Mutual Enterprises,* Manchester: Co-operatives UK, http://www.uk.coop/sites/default/files/co-operative_id.pdf, accessed 1st October 2012.

Balnave, N. and Patmore, G. (2013) 'Rochdale consumer co-operatives in Australia: decline and survival', *Business History,* 54: 986-1003.

BBC (1980) *The Mondragon Experiment,* London: British Broadcasting Corporation, (accessed 1st July 2013 http://www.youtube.com/watch?v=-obHJfTaQvw).

Birchall, J. (2009) *People-Centred Businesses,* Basingstoke: Palgrave Macmillan.

Birchall, J. (2012) 'A member-owned business approach to the classification of co-operatives and mutuals', in McDonnell, D. and MacKnight, E. (eds) (2012), *The Co-operative Model in Practice,* Glasgow: Co-operative Education Trust, pp. 67-82.

Bird, A. (2011) *Co-operation and Business Services – Finance as a Tool for Development,* Co-operatives and Mutuals Wales.

Borzaga, C. and Depedri, S. (2014) 'When social enterprises do it better: efficiency and efficacy of work integration in Italian social co-operatives', in S. Denny and F. Seddon (eds), *Social Enterprise: Accountability and Evaluation Around the World.* London: Routledge, pp. 85–101.

Boyd, I. (1974). 'Chesterton and Distributism', *New Blackfriars,* 55(649): 265-272.

Brown, J. (2006) 'Equity finance for social enterprises', *Social Enterprise Journal,* 2(1): 73-81.

Cathcart, A. (2009) *Directing Democracy: The Case of the John Lewis Partnership,* unpublished PhD Thesis, School of Management: University of Leicester.

Cathcart, A. (2014) 'Paradoxes of participation: non-union workplace partnership in John Lewis', *International Journal of Human Resource Management,* 25: 762-780.

Chell, E. (2007) 'Social enterprise and entrepreneurship: towards a convergent theory of the entrepreneurial process', *International Small Business Journal*, 25: 5-26.

Cooke, A. (1979) 'Robert Owen and the Stanley Mills, 1802-1811', *Business History*, 21: 107-11.

Coule, T. (2008) *Sustainability in Voluntary Organisations: Exploring the Dynamics of Organisational Strategy*, unpublished Thesis, Sheffield Hallam University.

Davidmann, M. (1996) *Co-op Study 7: Mondragon Co-operatives*, (accessed 27th June 2013).

Davies, P. (2002) *Introduction to Company Law*, Oxford: Oxford University Press.

Davies-Coates, J. (2014) 'Open co-ops: Inspiration, legal structures and tools", *Stir*, Issue 6, online at http://stirtoaction.com/open-co-ops-inspiration-legal-structures-and-tools/ (accessed 7th November 2014).

Davis, P. (2004). *Human Resource Management in Co-operatives: Theory, Process and Practice*. Co-operative Branch, International Labour Office, Geneva.

Dees, J. (1998) 'Enterprising non-profits: what do you do when traditional sources of funding fall short?' *Harvard Business Review*, Jan/Feb: 55-67.

Ellerman, D. (1984) 'Entrepreneurship in the Mondragon Co-operatives', *Review of Social Economy*, 42(3): 272-294.

Ellerman, D. (1990) *The Democratic Worker-Owned Firm: A New Model for East and West*, Boston: Unwin Hyman.

Ellerman, D. (2005) *Helping People Help Themselves: From the World Bank to an Alternative Philosophy of Development Assistance*, Ann Arbor: University of Michigan Press.

Emerson, J. and Twerksy, F. (1996) (eds) *New Social Entrepreneurs: The Success, Challenge and Lessons of Non-profit Enterprise Creation*. San Francisco: Roberts Foundation.

Erdal, D. (2000) *The Psychology of Sharing: An Evolutionary Approach*, unpublished PhD Thesis, University of St Andrews.

Erdal, D. (2009) *Local Heroes: How Loch Fyne Oysters Embraced Employee Ownership and Business Success*, London: Penguin.

Erdal, D. (2011) *Beyond the Corporation: Humanity Working*: London: The Bodley Head.

Golja, T. and Novkovic, S. 'Determinants of Cooperative Development in Croatia', In Ketilson, L. and Villettaz, M. (eds) *Cooperatives' Power to Innovation: Texts Selected from the International Call for Papers,* Levis: International Summit of Cooperatives, 2014, pp. 15-26.

Harrison, J. (1969) *Robert Owen and the Owenites in Britain and America,* London: Routledge and Kegan Paul.

Hawken, P. (2010) *The Ecology of Commerce: a Declaration of Sustainability,* New York: Harper Paperbacks.

Hayek, F. (1960) *The Constitution of Liberty,* London: Routledge and Kegan Paul.

Hayek, F. (1976) *Law, Legislation and Liberty: the Mirage of Social Justice,* London: Routledge and Kegan Paul.

Holyoake, G. (1858) *Self-Help by the People: The History of the Rochdale Pioneers 1844-1892,* 10th Edition, London: George Allen & Unwin, 1922. (accessed 1st July 2013 at http://gerald-massey.org.uk/holyoake/b_rochdale_index.htm).

Holyoake, G. (2013, [1877]) *The History of Co-operation,* Hardpress Publishing, 2013.

ICA/Euricse (2013) *The World Co-operative Monitor,* International Co-operative Alliance/Euricse, access at: http://www.monitor.coop.

Jain, P. 'Managing credit for the rural poor: lessons from the Grameen Bank', *World Development,* 24 (1996): 79-89.

Laasch, O. and Conway, R. (2015) *Principles of Responsible Management,* New York: Cengage.

Lewis, J.S. (1948) *Partnership for All: A Thirty Four Year Old Experiment in Industrial Democracy,* London: Kerr-Cross Publishing.

Lewis, J.S. (1954) *Fairer Shares: A Possible Advance in Civilization and Perhaps the Only Alternative to Communism,* London: Staples Press Ltd.

Lund, M. (2011) *Solidarity as a Business Model: A Multi-Stakeholder Co-operative's Manual,* Kent, OH: Cooperative Development Center, Kent State University.

Manwani, H. (2013) 'Profit's not always the point', *Ted Talk,* http://www.ted.com/talks/harish_manwani_profit_s_not_always_the_point?language=en, accessed 24th May 2015.

Martin, R. L. and Osberg, S. (2007) 'Social entrepreneurship: The case for definition', *Stanford Social Innovation Review*, Spring: 29-39.

Marx, K. and Engels, F. (1888) 'The communist manifesto' in *Works of Karl Marx and Friedrich Engels,* translated by Samuel Moore, downloaded from iBooks.

McDonnell, D., MacKnight, E. and Donnelly, H. (2012) *Democratic Enterprise: Ethical Business for the 21st Century,* Available at SSRN: http://ssrn.com/abstract=2041159.

McCulloch, M. and Ridley-Duff, R. (2015) 'Beyond Accounting for Capitals: FairShares – a model for recompensing capital contributions', in *Rethinking Capitals,* London: ICAEW, (in press).

Major, G. (1996) 'Solving the under-investment and degeneration problems of worker co-ops', *Annals of Public and Co-operative Economics,* 67: 545-601.

Major, G. (1998) 'The Need for NOVARS (Non-Voting Value Added Sharing Renewable Shares)', *Journal of Co-operative Studies,* 31(2): 57-72.

Major, G. and Boby, G. (2000) *Equity Devaluation, The Rarity of Democratic Firms, and 'Profit Shares',* www.democraticbusiness.co.uk/vanekps.html.

Melman, S. (2001) *After Capitalism: From Managerialism to Workplace Democracy,* New York: Alfred Knopf.

Molina, F. (2013) 'Fagor Electodomésticos: The multi-nationalisation of a Basque co-operative, 1955-2010', *Business History,* 54: 945 – 963.

Murray, R. (2011) *Co-operation in the Age of Google,* Manchester: Co-operatives UK, access at: http://www.uk.coop/ageofgoogle.

Nicholls, A. and Murdock, A. (2012) *Social Innovation: blurring boundaries to reconfigure markets*. Basingstoke: Palgrave Macmillan.

Nicholls, A. (ed.) (2006) *Social Entrepreneurship: New Models of Sustainable Social Change,* Oxford: Oxford University Press.

Norton, M. and Ariely, D. (2011), 'Building a Better America - a Wealth Quintile at a Time', *Perspectives on Psychological Science,* 6(1): 9 - 12.

Novkovic, S. and Webb, T. (2014) *Co-operatives in a Post-Growth Era: Creating Co-operative Economics*. London: Zed Books.

Oakeshott, R. (1990) *The Case for Worker Co-operatives*, 2nd Edition, Basingstoke: Palgrave Macmillan, [First Published 1978].

Owen, R. (1816) *A New View of Society*, Kindle Edition.

Paranque, B., & Willmott, H. (2014). 'Cooperatives: saviours or gravediggers of capitalism? The ambivalent case of the John Lewis Partnership', *Organization,* 21(5): 604-625.

Parnell, E. (2011) *Co-operation: The Beautiful Idea*, Los Gatos, CA: Smashwords.

Pérotin, V. and Robinson, A. (eds), (2004) *Employee Participation, Firm Performance and Survival*, Oxford: Elsevier.

Perrini, F. and Vurro, C. (2006) 'Social entrepreneurship: Innovation and social change across theory and practice'. In Mair J., Robinson J. and Hockerts K. (eds), *Social Entrepreneurship*, London: Palgrave Macmillan, pp. 57-85.

Roelants, B., Hyungsik, E. and Terassi, E. (2014) *Cooperatives and Employment: A Global Report*. Quebec: CICOPA/Desjardin.

Porter, M. and Kramer, M. (2011) 'Creating shared value', *Harvard Business Review*, Jan-Feb: 2 – 17.

Restakis, J. (2010) *Humanizing the Economy: Co-operatives in the Age of Capital*. Gabriola Island: New Society Publishers.

Ridley-Duff, R. J. and Bull, M. (2011) *Understanding Social Enterprise: Theory and Practice*, London: Sage Publications.

Ridley-Duff, R. and Bull, M. (2013) "The FairShares Model: a communitarian pluralist approach to social enterprise development?" paper to 34th ISBE Conference, Cardiff, 6 – 8 Nov.

Ridley-Duff, R. and Bull, M. (2014) "The (hidden) origins of a social enterprise movement: a communitarian pluralist perspective?" submission to Business History, December 2014,

Ridley-Duff, R. and Bull, M. (2015) *Understanding Social Enterprise: Theory and Practice*, 2nd Edition, London: Sage Publications, (in press).

Ridley-Duff, R. J. and Southcombe, C. (2012) 'The Social Enterprise Mark: a critical review of its conceptual dimensions', *Social Enterprise Journal*, 8(3): 178-200, http://shura.shu.ac.uk/5571/.

Ridley-Duff, R. J., Southcombe, C. and Dickins, N. (2013) *The FairShares Model*, Sheffield: FairShares Association, http://shura.shu.ac.uk/6635/.

Ridley-Duff, R. J. (2005) *Communitarian Perspectives on Corporate Governance*, PhD Thesis, Sheffield Hallam University, http://shura.shu.ac.uk/2681/.

Ridley-Duff, R. J. (2007) 'Communitarian perspectives on social enterprise', *Corporate Governance: An International Review*, 15(2): 382-392, http://shura.shu.ac.uk/721/.

Ridley-Duff, R. J. (2008) 'Social enterprise as a socially rational business', *International Journal of Entrepreneurial Behaviour and Research*, 14(5): 291-312, http://shura.shu.ac.uk/2680/.

Ridley-Duff, R. J. (2009) 'Cooperative social enterprises: company rules, access to finance and management practice', *Social Enterprise Journal*, 5(1): 50-68, http://shura.shu.ac.uk/774/.

Ridley-Duff, R. J. (2010) 'Communitarian governance in social enterprises: case evidence from the Mondragon Co-operative Corporation and School Trends Ltd', *Social Enterprise Journal*, 6(2): 125-145, http://shura.shu.ac.uk/1714/.

Ridley-Duff, R. J. (2012a) 'New frontiers in democratic self-management', in McDonnell, D. and MacKnight, E. (eds), *The Co-operative Model in Practice*, Glasgow: Co-operative Education Trust, pp. 99-117, http://shura.shu.ac.uk/7104/

Ridley-Duff, R. J. (2012b) *Creative Commons*, discussion paper for the *School for Democratic Socialism* and *Co-operative Party*.

Ridley-Duff, R. (2015) "The FairShares Model: an ethical approach to social enterprise development?" *Econviews*, (in press), http://shura.shu.ac.uk/9672/

Robertson, A. (1969) 'Robert Owen and the Campbell Debt 1810-1822', *Business History*, 11: 23-30.

Rodrick, S. (2005) *Leveraged ESOPs and Employee Buyouts*, Oakland, CA: The National Center for Employee Ownership.

Rothschild, J., and Allen-Whitt, J. (1986) *The Co-operative Workplace*. Cambridge: Cambridge University Press.

SHU (2014) *Democratising Co-operatives, Charities and Social Enterprises*, REF Impact Case, Sheffield Hallam University, http://impact.ref.ac.uk/CaseStudies/CaseStudy.aspx?Id=4965.

Toms, S. (2012) 'Producer co-operatives and economic efficiency: Evidence from the nineteenth century cotton textile industry', *Business History*, 54: 855-882.

Turnbull, S. (1994), 'Stakeholder democracy: redesigning the governance of firms and bureaucracies', *Journal of Socio-Economics*, 23(3): 321-360.

Turnbull, S. (1995) 'Innovations in corporate governance: The Mondragon Experience', *Corporate Governance: An International Review*, 3(3): 167-180.

Turnbull, S. (2002) *A New Way to Govern: Organisations and Society after Enron*, London: New Economics Foundation.

Uphoff, N., Esman, M. and Krishna, A. (1998) *Reasons for Success: Learning from Instructive Experiences in Rural Development*, West Hartford, CT: Kumarian.

Vanek, J. (1970) *The General Theory of Labor-Managed Market Economies*, Ithaca: Cornell University.

Vieta, M., (2010) 'The New Co-operativism'. *Affinities*, 4(1): online http://journals.sfu.ca/affinities/index.php/affinities/issue/view/4/showToc.

Westall, A. (2001) *Value-Led, Market-Driven: Social Enterprise Solutions to Public Policy Goals*, London: IPPR.

Wilkinson, R. and Pickett, K. (2010) *The Spirit Level: Why Equality is Better for Everyone*, London: Penguin.

Whyte, W. and Whyte, K. (1991) *Making Mondragon*, New York: ILR Press/Itchaca.

Wilson, M., Shaw, L. and Lonergan, G. (2012) *Our Story: Rochdale Pioneers Museum*, Rochdale: Co-operative Heritage Trust, www.rochdalepioneersmuseum.coop.

Young, C. and Dworkin, M. (2013) *Shift Change*, Moving Images, www.shiftchange.org.

Yunus, M. (2007) *Creating a World without Poverty*, New York: Public Affairs.

Key Working Papers on FairShares

Ridley-Duff, R. and Bull, M. (2013) "The FairShares Model: a communitarian pluralist approach to social enterprise development?" paper to 34th ISBE Conference, Cardiff, 6 – 8 Nov.

Ridley-Duff, R. and Bull, M. (2014) "The (hidden) origins of a social enterprise movement: a communitarian pluralist perspective?" submission to Business History, December 2014.

Ridley-Duff, R. (2015) "The FairShares Model: an ethical approach to social enterprise development?" *Econviews*, (in press), http://shura.shu.ac.uk/9672/.

Rory Ridley-Duff

Part 2 – Educating for Change

If you were engaged and enthused by Part 1, you can act on your enthusiasm in Part 2. In this part of the book, I have reproduced learning materials created with Mike Bull for the textbook *Understanding Social Enterprise: Theory and Practice (USE)*. We are amazed at how popular this book has become (all over the world) as both a reader for academics and as a textbook for under-graduate and post-graduate education. Here is a brief description of what you can expect.

The teaching materials have been informed by action research projects to help social enterprises and social entrepreneurs develop their social enterprise management skills. Mike's Balance Diagnostics sit alongside FairShares Diagnostics as tools designed to influence and change practice. We are both concerned to help develop inclusive management styles and enhance practitioners' capacity to benefit from improvements in workplace democracy.

Part 2 includes activities in which you use all the FairShares Social Auditing Tools and Advanced Diagnostics included in *FairShares Model* V2.1. Activities 2.1 to 2.7 take you through Levels 1 and 2 of the *FairShares Model*. Activities 2.8 to 2.11 are more challenging, aimed at advancing member, governor and executive education. Activities 2.12 and 2.13 are projects that can be pursued by practitioners (2.12) and scholars (2.13) to generate advanced knowledge of FairShares. Please enjoy, refine and feedback your experiences to the FairShares Online Community.

Summary of learning activities

2.1 – Your Social Enterprise Values (USE Chapter 2)
2.2 – Level 1 FairShares Social Audit (USE Chapter 8).
2.3 – Level 1 FairShares Participation Audit (USE Chapter 8).
2.4 – Level 1 FairShares Governance Audit (USE Chapter 12).
2.5 – Advanced Management Diagnostics
2.6 – Advanced Participation Diagnostics
2.7 – Advanced Governance Diagnostics
2.8 - Reviewing the Governance Diagnostics
2.9 – Using FairShares to End Exploitation
2.10 - Combatting Wealth Inequality with FairShares
2.11 – Role Play: Taking Big Decisions
2.12 - Building a Solidarity Enterprise
2.13 - Building a FairShares course curriculum

Activity 2.1 – Your social enterprise values

This survey – often the first to be used in beginning a course on social enterprise – gives students a chance to consider statements that have been made about social enterprise, and the extent to which they describe the social enterprises they have encountered. Below we reproduce the survey on paper and also provide URLs to an online version that can be used in classroom teaching.

Guidance

This survey presents eighteen statements about social enterprise from five widely used definitions. The list of characteristics were compiled for an academic paper by Rory Ridley-Duff and Cliff Southcombe that was published in 2012.

In this survey, you can express your view on the prevalence of these characteristics within the wider social economy. To assess how deeply embedded they are in a specific enterprise, you can use the FairShares Advanced Management Diagnostics after completing this survey.

There are three groups of questions that correspond to the three domains of practice identified by Social Enterprise Europe:

- Social Purpose and Impact
- Ethics and Values
- Socialised and Democratic Ownership, Governance and Management

The survey normally takes up to 15 minutes. I include questions for debate and discussion after the survey.

Distance Learning - This survey is online at:

http://www.fairshares.coop/social-enterprise-survey.

Results can updated in real time in the classroom.

Survey Page 1 - Social Purpose and Impact

Below are six statements that describe the scope and depth of social value creation in the social economy. You will initially give your view of the scope of each statement, then rank them in order of importance to you.

Q. *Choose the answers that most closely reflect your view on the social purpose and impact of social enterprises.*

Statements	None	Some	Most	All
A social enterprise provides evidence that it makes a positive social impact and/or runs for community benefit				
A social enterprise makes clear statements about its social and/or environmental purposes/objectives				
A social enterprise provides at least some paid employment				
A social enterprise provides education/training to its members, managers, workforce and elected representatives				
A social enterprise continuously produces and/or sells goods and services to improve well-being				
A social enterprise reinvests most of its surplus/profit back into its social/environmental purpose				

Q. *Please rank the above statements in the order they are important to you.*

Statements	Rank

A social enterprise provides evidence that it makes a positive social impact and/or runs for community benefit

A social enterprise makes clear statements about its social and/or environmental purposes/objectives

A social enterprise provides at least some paid employment

A social enterprise provides education/training to its members, managers, workforce and elected representatives

A social enterprise continuously produces and/or sells goods and services to improve well-being

A social enterprise reinvests most of its surplus/profit back into its social/environmental purpose

Survey Page 2 – Ethics and Values

Below are six statements that describe ethical positions you could take in the social economy. You will initially give your view of the scope of each statement, then rank them in order of importance to you.

Q. *Please choose the answer that most closely matches your views on the ethics and values of social enterprises.*

Statements	None	Some	Most	All
A social enterprise states (and reviews) its ethical values and principles				
A social enterprise ensures that most (or all) of its assets are used for community/public benefit				

Statements	None	Some	Most	All
A social enterprise is created through the actions of citizens voluntarily working together to meet a need				
A social enterprise receives most of its income from trading activities, not grants or donations				
A social enterprise discourages a 'for-profit' mind set by limiting the distribution of surpluses/profits for private benefit				
A social enterprise balances member (stakeholder) needs with sustainable community development				

Q. *Please rank the above statements in the order they are important to you.*

Statements	Rank
A social enterprise states (and reviews) its ethical values and principles	
A social enterprise ensures that most (or all) of its assets are used for community/public benefit	
A social enterprise is created through the actions of citizens voluntarily working together to meet a need	
A social enterprise receives most of its income from trading activities, not grants or donations	
A social enterprise discourages a 'for-profit' mind-set by limiting the distribution of surpluses/profits for private benefit	
A social enterprise balances member (stakeholder) needs with sustainable community development	

Survey Page 3 - Ownership, Management and Governance

Finally, below are six statements that describe issues related to ownership, management and governance in the social economy. You will initially give your view of the scope of each statement, then rank them in order of importance to you.

Q. *Please choose the answers that most closely reflects your views on ownership, management and governance in social enterprises.*

	None	Some	Most	All
A social enterprise educates the public about the benefits of its business model				
A social enterprise is not owned or controlled by a private company or public authority				
A social enterprise encourages capital contributions by members (and offers them a social and/or economic return).				
A social enterprise continuously encourages cooperative working / networking				
A social enterprise opens up ownership and/or membership to primary stakeholders (workforce, customers and/or service users)				
A social enterprise is governed by one or more of its primary stakeholders (workforce, customers and/or service users)				

Q. Please rank the above statements in the order they are important to you.

Statements	Rank
A social enterprise educates the public about the benefits of its business model	
A social enterprise is not owned or controlled by a private company or public authority	
A social enterprise encourages capital contributions by members (and offers them a social and/or economic return).	
A social enterprise continuously encourages cooperative working / networking	
A social enterprise opens up ownership and/or membership to primary stakeholders (workforce, customers and/or service users	
A social enterprise is governed by one or more of its primary stakeholders (workforce, customers and/or service users)	

Q. Now write below a definition of social enterprise that enables it to be distinguished from a public body, private company and non-profit organisation.

Copyright Rory Ridley-Duff, Cliff Southcombe and Natasha Ridley-Duff, Creative Commons 4.0 - BY-NC-SA

Questions

Q: Which characteristics do you believe 'All' and 'Most' social enterprises share?

Q: Which characteristics have you rated as the most important to you?

Q: Do the two lists match?

Q: If not, why do they differ?

Activity 2.2 – Level 1 social audit

A Level 1 Social Audit can be used to determine which 'level' of FairShares an organisation has implemented.

Level 0   The organisation does not subscribe to FairShares values and principles (see Appendix A).

Level 1   The organisation disseminates information about FairShares Values and Principles but does not practice them in its own ownership, governance and management.

Level 2   The organisation subscribes to FairShares values and principles and has implemented them using its own proprietary system of ownership, governance and management.

Level 3   The organisation subscribes to FairShares values and principles and has implemented them through using FairShares Association IP for ownership, governance and management.

Take up to 10 minutes to interview the person sitting next to you using the following social auditing questions.

Initial Social Audit

(Interview / Focus Group Questions)

Purpose and Impact

(PRME Principle – Sustainability)

This section asks you to explain the social value that your organisation creates, and how you know that this value has been created.

1. What is the purpose of your enterprise?
2. How is the social, environmental and economic impact of your trading assessed?

Ethics and Values

(PRME Principle – Ethics)

This section is about the values and principles that guide you on:

- **what** to produce
- the **way** you produce and deliver them
- the **way** you *sell* them (if appropriate)

For the first question, consider what motivates you to offer what you offer. For the second question, consider what motivates you to treat staff, customers, clients and users in the way that you do.

3. What values and principles guide the choice of goods/services that you offer?
4. What values and principles guide the way you produce and/or sell those goods and services?

Ownership, Management and Governance

(PRME Principle – Responsibility)

This section asks you identify the groups ('primary stakeholders') without which your organisation could not function. For example, an education provider could not exist without at least one teacher and some students. You are then asked how you achieve equitable outcomes for all your primary stakeholders. For example, you can describe systems you have devised for sharing wealth and power in a way that satisfies everyone.

5. Who are your primary (secondary and tertiary) stakeholders?
6. How do the ownership, governance and management systems ensure an equitable distribution of wealth and power to all primary stakeholders?

Copyright 2014, Rory Ridley-Duff, Cliff Southcombe, Nicci Dickins and Natasha Ridley-Duff, Creative Commons 4.0 - BY-NC-SA

Question

Q: What is this organisation's level of alignment with FairShares values and principles? (Appendix A).

Distance Learning: students can do this activity online:

www.fairshares.coop/initial-social-audit

Use the Learning and Teaching version.

Additional support documentation is available on the FairShares Wiki. To study these issues quantitatively, use the Advanced Management Diagnostics later in this chapter (and online).

Activity 2.3 – Level 1 participation audit

A Level 1 Participation Audit can be used to determine the 'depth' of workforce participation.

Depth 1	**No Involvement**: a management style where members/ employees are not invited to meetings or elected to management bodies to contribute to operational or strategic decision-making. Typically, staff are not provided with any verbal or written guidance by managers and/or governors before decisions are made.
Depth 2	**Passive involvement**: a management style where members/ employees are provided with both written and verbal guidance by managers and/or governors, but are not invited or elected (individually or in groups) to contribute to operational or strategic decision-making.
Depth 3	**Active Involvement**: a management style where members/ employees (individually or in groups) have discussions about (pre-formed) management proposals,

	but are not invited or elected to participate in the formation of these proposals, or final decisions about their implementation.
Depth 4	**Managed Participation**: a management style where members/ employees (individually or in groups) can participate in the development of ideas, and where managers focus on coaching members/employees to develop their ideas into proposals, and support them during implementation. Managers retain some powers to screen out weak proposals.
Depth 5	**Member-Driven Participation:** a management style where any member/employee (individually or in groups) can initiate discussions on operational or strategic issues, arrange and participate in meetings to develop proposals, and exercise both voice and voting power when decisions are made about implementation.

Take up to 15 minutes to interview the person sitting next to you using the following participation auditing questions.

Distance Learning: Students can undertake this activity online by opening the URL:

www.fairshares.coop/initial-participation-audit

(Use the Learning and Teaching version).

Initial Participation Audit

(Interview / Focus Group Questions)

Purpose and Impact

(PRME Principle – Sustainability)

This section asks you about your participation in creating social purpose and impact. An enterprise creates its purpose and impact through designing products and services. Individually, people at work have appraisals to work out their own contribution to the purpose and impact of their organisation. Sustainable production is achieved when an organisation does not use resources more quickly than they can be replaced.

1. How do you want to participate in designing new products and services?
2. How do you want to participate in getting your products and services to the people who need them?
3. How do you want to participate in staff (member) appraisals?
4. How do you want to participate in ensuring products and services are sustainably produced?

Ethics and Values

(PRME Principle – Ethics)

This section asks you three questions. When people learn at work, they are learning more than technical skills - they are also learning social skills.

- The first question explores how you want to be treated (and how you want others to be treated) **when learning new skills** at work.
- The second question explores which ethics and values you want to guide **the process of appointment** to new positions.
- The third question explores the values and principles that you want to guide the treatment of people **on a day-to-day basis.**

5. What would encourage you (and those around you) to participate in learning new skills?
6. What ethics should be applied to the process of appointing / electing staff (members) to new positions?
7. How would you like to be treated (and others be treated) while you are doing your day-to-day work?

Democratic Ownership, Management and Governance

(PRME Principle – Responsibility)

This section contains three questions about your participation in managing the wealth creation of your organisation.

- The first question explores how you want to be involved in **developing the long-term goals** of your organisation.
- The second question explores how you would like to participate in **setting the terms and conditions** of employment.
- The third question explores your role in creating a fair system for **allocating surpluses and deficits**.

8. How do you want to participate in planning for the medium and long term?

9. How do you want to participate in setting wages, hours and leave entitlements?

10. How do you want to participate in allocating surpluses (profits) and deficits (losses)?

Copyright 2014, Rory Ridley-Duff, Alistair Ponton, Natasha Ridley-Duff and Viewpoint Research CIC, Creative Commons 4.0 - BY-NC-SA

Question

Q: Which level of workforce participation do you believe is currently occurring in this place of work?

You can study these issues using quantitative survey tools. See the Advanced Participation Diagnostics activity later in this chapter and online. Additional support document is available on the FairShares Wiki

Activity 2.4 – Level 1 governance audit

A Level 1 Governance Audit can be used to determine the governance orientation of an organisation through a series of questions about its internal and external relationships.

Orientations toward governance are theorised as follows:

2.1 – Governance orientations

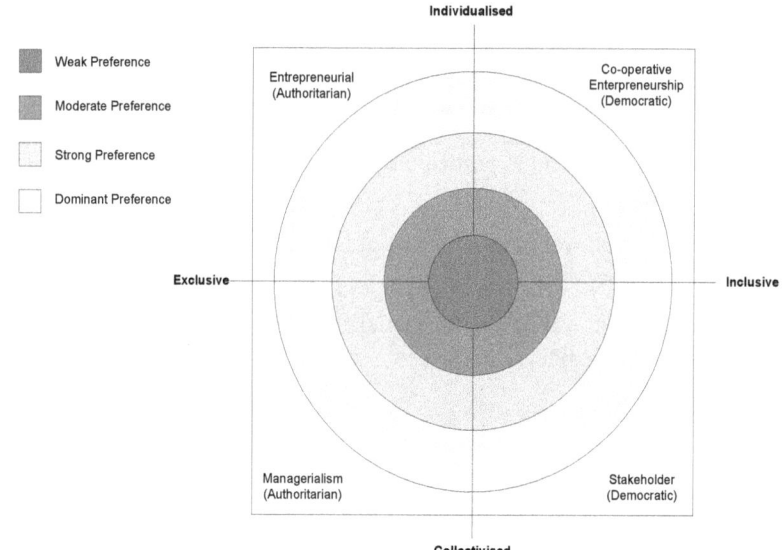

Copyright Rory Ridley-Duff, Tracey Coule, Mike Bull,
Creative Commons 4.0 - BY-NC-SA

Each orientation has a description attached. We recommend you read these before you begin the initial governance audit.

> **Distance Learning**: students can do this survey by opening the following URL:
>
> www.fairshares.coop/initial-governance-audit
>
> Use the Learning and Teaching version.

Entrepreneurialism

(individualised exclusive)

Governance dominated by a recognised leader to whom others defer and whose values dominate in decision-making, disputes and communications. Rules are created when the leader needs to resolve a dispute or re-establish their authority. The leader allocates responsibilities (and adjudicates conflicts) or delegates the authority to a person they trust. The leader takes an entrepreneurial approach to decision-making, selects / appoints senior management to meet goals set, then runs the organisation on the assumption that they have control rights. Both entrepreneur-led enterprises (social and private) as well as charities established by a philanthropist or political activist can take on this character. One upside is fast efficient action that is targeted according the values/vision of the entrepreneur. A downside, however, is that the entrepreneur (or those they favour) may not adequately consider the needs or views of those outside their peer group.

Managerialism

(collectivised / exclusive)

Governance by a managerial elite who are able to create or impose a consensus. Rules reflect their shared values and they allocate responsibilities and adjudicate disputes according to their perception of collective interests ("the common good"). Elites sometimes take their authority for granted and entrench their right to make appointments and key decisions. Authority is based on educational or professional qualifications, 'expert' status in a particular field, and/or perceived social status (as indicated by formal/informal hierarchies). In addition, businesses started by families, work colleagues or closely knit social networks may develop in this way. Lastly, co-operatives and mutual societies with an **inactive** membership can start to adopt similar practices. One upside is the cohesion of the dominant group and the shared values that can lead to focussed and effective action. One downside, however, is that points of views held by non-professionals or those with low perceived social status can become marginalized or ignored, leading to oppressive cultures that resist change.

Co-operative entrepreneurship

(individualised inclusive)

Governance that encourages individual initiative and accommodates conflict through respect for individual rights and commitment to dialogue. Balance is achieved through democratic approaches to control based on individual action and devolved responsibilities. One-member / one-vote societies, associations, democratic businesses and co-operatives may show a preference for this approach (or profess commitment to it). Directors and executive officers may be elected by the membership rather than appointed by an elite. Overall, there is an emphasis on egalitarianism and individual action, rather than corporate control. One upside of this approach is the reported level of individual commitment and satisfaction amongst members and employees, leading to adaptability and innovation when change is needed. One downside, however, arises when trying to reach agreement with other organisations that want to negotiate with a 'leader' rather than a collective.

Stakeholder Democracy

(Collectivised / Inclusive)

Governance that recognises group interests and promotes debate / discussion between stakeholders throughout the organisation. Conflict is accommodated through debate and negotiation rather than the imposition of rules and centralised controls. Social and economic challenges are met with a mixture of participation at team level and representative democracy at senior levels. Directors, managers and executive officers may (in some cases) be elected and removed by their groups rather than appointed / co-opted by board members. One upside of this approach is the acknowledgement and recognition of group interests as well as the responsiveness of senior staff to the needs of different stakeholders. One downside, however, may be the time it takes to reach consensus across the organisation as underlying group interests create additional challenges and conflicts.

Using the initial governance audit

This survey presents six invitations to describe an organisation's governance system. The open questions constitute an initial FairShares Governance Audit. You can explore your findings in more detail using the Advanced Governance Diagnostics.

These six invitations explore awareness of relationships that influence governance in an organisation. They explore your awareness of relationships affecting:

- The regulators who oversee your type of enterprise
- Your suppliers, clients and beneficiaries
- Your funders and/or investors
- Your workforce (both voluntary and paid)
- Your executive team
- Your board's development

Take whatever time you need (subject to lecture constraints) to interview the person sitting next. Your goal is to develop a 'rich picture' of their approach to governance.

Initial Governance Audit
(Interview / Focus Group Questions)

External Relations
Organisations have internal and external stakeholders. In this section we ask you about external stakeholders:
- regulating authorities
- customers
- users
- suppliers
- beneficiaries
- funders
- institutional investors

1. Describe the regulatory authorities you have to deal with, and how you manage your relationships with them.
2. Describe some of the challenges in managing relationships with customers, users, suppliers and beneficiaries.
3. Describe the business model you've developed (or are developing) to generate the funds you need to achieve your social objectives.

Internal Relations

This section asks you about the groups that comprise your workforce.
- employees
- volunteers
- member-owners
- managers
- directors / trustees

4. Describe the composition of your workforce, and the challenges you face in attracting, retaining and developing it.
5. Describe the differences between 'management' and 'administration' (or are they the same thing)?
6. How do the responsibilities of board members, managers and owners differ from each other (if at all)?

Copyright 2014, Rory Ridley-Duff, Tracey Coule, Mike Bull, Natasha Ridley-Duff, Creative Commons 4.0 - BY-NC-SA

Question

Q. Which orientation(s) do you believe are guiding the governance of this organisation?

If you want to study these issues using quantitative survey instruments, see the Advanced Governance Diagnostics activity later in this chapter and online. Additional support documentation is available on the FairShares Wiki

Activity 2.5 – Advanced management diagnostics

This survey – designed for use after an Initial Social Audit – enables a group of people to collectively take a view of how their social values are put into practice. The list of characteristics are the same as the Social Enterprise Values Survey (Activity 2.1) but instead of considering social enterprises in general, respondents answer about their own organisation. We reproduce the survey in the book and provide URLs to an online version for classroom teaching and distance learning.

Guidance

This survey presents eighteen statements about social enterprise that have been used to aid its definition. The list of characteristics were compiled for an academic paper by Rory Ridley-Duff and Cliff Southcombe in 2012.

In this survey, you can express your view on how deeply embedded these characteristics are in an enterprise (social or otherwise). There are three groups of questions that correspond to the three domains of practice identified by Social Enterprise Europe:

- Social Purpose and Impact
- Ethics and Values
- Socialised (Democratic) Ownership, Governance and Management

The survey normally takes 5 - 10 minutes.

> **Distance learning**: students can complete the Advanced Management Diagnostics online using the following URL:
>
> www.fairshares.coop/advanced-management-diagnostics
>
> Use the Learning and Teaching version.

Survey Page 1 - Social Purpose and Impact

Below are six statements that describe the scope and depth of social value creation in an enterprise that you name. You will initially give your view of the scope of each statement, then rank them in order of importance to people in the enterprise.

Name of your enterprise:

Q. *Choose answers that reflect the prevalence of management practices listed below in this enterprise.*

Statements	Never / Rarely	Occasionally	Frequently	Routinely
This enterprise provides evidence that it makes a positive social impact and/or runs for community benefit				
This enterprise makes clear statements about its social and/or environmental purposes/objectives				
This enterprise provides at least some paid employment				
This enterprise provides education/training to its members, managers, workforce and elected representatives				
This enterprise continuously produces and/or sells goods and services to improve well-being				
This enterprise reinvests most of its surplus/profit back into its social/environmental purpose				

Q. *Please rank the above statements in the order you think they are important to people in the enterprise.*

Statements	Rank
This enterprise provides evidence that it makes a positive social impact and/or runs for community benefit	
This enterprise makes clear statements about its social and/or environmental purposes/objectives	
This enterprise provides at least some paid employment	
This enterprise provides education/training to its members, managers, workforce and elected representatives	
This enterprise continuously produces and/or sells goods and services to improve well-being	
This enterprise reinvests most of its surplus/profit back into its social/environmental purpose	

Survey Page 2 – Ethics and Values

Below are six statements that describe ethical positions you could take in running this enterprise. You will initially give your view of the scope of each statement, then rank them in order of importance to people in this enterprise.

Q. *Please choose the answer that reflect the prevalence of management practices in this enterprise.*

Statements	Never / Rarely	Occasionally	Frequently	Routinely
This enterprise states (and reviews) its ethical values and principles				
This enterprise ensures that most (or all) of its assets are used for community/public benefit				

Statements	Never / Rarely	Occasionally	Frequently	Routinely
This enterprise is created through the actions of citizens voluntarily working together to meet a need				
This enterprise receives most of its income from trading activities, not grants or donations				
This enterprise discourages a 'for-profit' mind set by limiting the distribution of surpluses/profits for private benefit				
This enterprise balances member (stakeholder) needs with sustainable community development				

Q. *Please rank the above statements in the order they are important to people in this enterprise.*

Statements	Rank
This enterprise states (and reviews) its ethical values and principles	
This enterprise ensures that most (or all) of its assets are used for community/public benefit	
This enterprise is created through the actions of citizens voluntarily working together to meet a need	
This enterprise receives most of its income from trading activities, not grants or donations	
This enterprise discourages a 'for-profit' mind-set by limiting the distribution of surpluses/profits for private benefit	
This enterprise balances member (stakeholder) needs with sustainable community development	

Survey Page 3 - Ownership, Management and Governance

Finally, below are six statements that describe issues related to ownership, management and governance in the social economy. You will initially give your view of the scope of each statement, then rank them in order of importance to people in the enterprise.

Q. *Please choose the answers that reflect the prevalence of the management practices listed below in this enterprise.*

Statements	Never / Rarely	Occasionally	Frequently	Routinely
This enterprise educates the public about the benefits of its business model				
This enterprise is not owned or controlled by a private company or public authority				
This enterprise encourages capital contributions by members (and offers them a social and/or economic return).				
This enterprise continuously encourages cooperative working / networking				
This enterprise opens up ownership and/or membership to primary stakeholders (workforce, customers and/or service users)				
This enterprise is governed by one or more of its primary stakeholders (workforce, customers and/or service users)				

Educating for Change

Q. Please rank the above statements in the order they are important to people in this organisation.

Statements   **Rank**

This enterprise educates the public about the benefits of its business model

This enterprise is not owned or controlled by a private company or public authority

This enterprise encourages capital contributions by members (and offers them a social and/or economic return).

This enterprise continuously encourages cooperative working / networking

This enterprise opens up ownership and/or membership to primary stakeholders (workforce, customers and/or service users

This enterprise is governed by one or more of its primary stakeholders (workforce, customers and/or service users)

Q. (Optional) Now write a statement on the social value that you think this enterprise creates.

Copyright Rory Ridley-Duff, Cliff Southcombe and Natasha Ridley-Duff, Creative Commons 4.0 - BY-NC-SA

Questions

Q: Which do you do 'Frequently' and 'Routinely'?

Q: Which characteristics have you rated as the most important to you?

Q: Do the two lists match?

Q: If not, why are they different?

Additional support documentation is available on the FairShares Wiki.

Activity 2.6 – Advanced participation diagnostics

This activity allows you to follow up use of the Initial Participation Audit by using survey tools that allow for the identification of work areas where the workforce would like more (or less) participation in management.

Guidance

This survey presents ten pairs of questions that help to investigate workforce (member) depth of participation in organisation development (see Activity 2.3). The pairs of questions are presented in three groups to reflect domains of practice identified by Social Enterprise Europe:

- Social Purpose and Impact
- Ethics and Values
- Socialised (Democratic) Ownership, Governance and Management

The advanced workforce participation diagnostics normally take 10 - 15 minutes to complete. In all cases, choose the answers that are closest to your own views.

Distance learning: students can complete the survey online using the following URL:

www.fairshares.coop/advanced-participation-diagnostics/

Use the Learning and Teaching version.

Page 1 - Social Purpose and Impact

This section asks you about your participation in creating social purpose and impact.

An enterprise creates its purpose and impact through designing products and services. Individually, people at work have appraisals to work out their own contribution to the purpose and impact of their organisation. Sustainable production is achieved when an organisation does not use resources more quickly than they can be replenished.

Choose the answers that are closest to your own views.

Q1. How do you want to participate in designing this organisation's products and services?

My colleagues / I...	How is it now?	How would you like it to be?
1) ...don't want to be (or are not allowed to be) involved.		
2) ...get given information about product / service developments.		
3) ...discuss product / service initiatives before managers finalise them.		
4) ...can implement proposals if we get management support		
5) ...can make proposals and participate in implementing decisions.		

Can't choose answers? What to comment more? Please say why...

Q2. **How do you want to participate in getting your products and services to the people who need them (i.e. developing viable markets)?**

My colleagues / I...	How is it now?	What would be your ideal?
1) ...don't want to be (or are not allowed to be) involved in market development.		
2) ...get informed by managers about new market development activity.		
3) ...discuss new marketing initiatives with managers before implementation.		
4) ...make marketing proposals and seek managers' support to implement them.		
5) ...make marketing proposals and/or participate in decisions about them		

Q3. **How do you want to participate in staff / member appraisals?**

My colleagues / I...	How is it now?	What would be your ideal?
1) ...don't want to be appraised (or don't have appraisals).		
2) ...get given information about appraisals before they take place.		
3) ...discuss the appraisal process with a manager before it takes place.		
4) ...control our career choices in collaboration with managers.		
5) ...choose our own career paths and decide who to involve in our appraisals.		

Can't choose answers? Want the say more? Please say why...

Q4. How do you want to participate in ensuring our products and services are sustainably produced?

My colleagues / I...	How is it now?	What would be your ideal?
1) ...have no influence on (or don't have an interest in) sustainability.		
2) ...listen to our managers' ideas on sustainable sourcing.		
3) ...actively contribute to managers' proposals for sustainable sourcing.		
4) ...make proposals on sustainability and get input from managers.		
5) ...develop and implement sustainability policies for our area(s) of responsibility.		

Can't choose answers? What to comment more? Please say why...

Page 2 – Ethics and Values

This section asks you three more questions. When people learn at work, they are learning more than technical skills - they are also learning social skills.

The first question explores how you want to participate (and how you want others to be treated) when learning new skills at work. The second question explores how you want to participate in the process of induction for people appointed to new positions. The third question explores the way you want to participate in decisions about day-to-day operations.

Choose the answers that are closest to your views.

Q5. What values should be prioritised when developing new skills?

My colleagues / I...	How is it now?	How would you like it to be?
1) ...learn on the job. No formal training is given / required.		
2) ...get training / instruction from managers when skills need developing.		
3) ...meet to discuss managers' training plan(s) before making final decisions.		
4) ...invite managers to listen to our training plans and contribute to implementation.		
5) ...can propose training plans and participate in any decisions about them.		

Can't choose answers? Want the say more? Please say why...

Q6. What attitude would you like to encourage toward staff inductions?

My colleagues / I...	How is it now?	How would you like it to be?
1) ...shouldn't be involved (or are excluded from involvement).		
2) ...will brief new staff and provide feedback if a manager asks.		
3) ...are involved in discussing managers' proposals for inducting our staff.		
4) ...implement our proposals for inducting staff (if managers are supportive).		
5) ...manage all aspects of inducting new staff into our work group.		

Q7. What values do you want to guide operational (day-to-day) decision-making?

My colleagues / I...	How is it now?	How would you like it to be?
1) ...leave operational problems for managers to deal with.		
2) ... raise issues so managers can decide how to act on them.		
3) ...can comment on management ideas before they finalise a solution.		
4) ...present ideas / solutions and involve managers in implementing them.		
5) ...generate ideas, implement solutions and involve others when needed.		

Can't choose answers? Want to say more? Please say why...

Page 3 - Ownership, Governance and Management

This section contains three questions about your participation in managing the wealth creation of your organisation. The first question explores how you want to be involved in developing the long-term goals of your organisation. The second question explores how you would like to participate in setting the terms and conditions of work. The third question explores your role in creating a fair system for allocating surpluses and deficits.

Choose answers that are closest to your views.

Q8. How do you want to participate in planning for the medium and long-term?

My colleagues / I...	How is it now?	How would you like it to be?
1) ...don't want to (or can't) participate in strategic planning.		
2) ...meet with a manager when they want to tell us their strategic plans.		
3) ...meet with managers to discuss plans before final decisions are made.		
4) ...seek managers' input on our strategic plan(s) to help us choose the best.		
5) ...can initiate a strategy and organise discussions / decisions on it.		

Can't choose answers? Want the say more? Please say why...

Q9. How do you want to participate in allocating surpluses (profits) and deficits (losses)?

My colleagues / I...	How is it now?	How would you like it to be?
1) ...just want a regular pay packet (or have no chance to discuss this).		
2) ...appreciate being told about the current / future system for this.		
3) ...contribute ideas before managers makes any final decisions.		
4) ...propose profit / loss sharing systems with input from a manager.		
5) ...devise profit / loss sharing systems and decide how to implement them.		

Q10. How do you want to participate in setting wages, hours and leave entitlements?

My colleagues / I...	How is it now?	How would you like it to be?
1) ...don't get informed by managers about changes to conditions of employment.		
2) ...receive information from managers about changes to employment terms.		
3) ...discuss changes to employment terms before final decisions are made.		
4) ...can propose working conditions and negotiate with managers (via a union).		
5) ...can propose new working conditions and agree them with colleagues.		

Can't choose answers? Want the say more? Please say why...

Questions

Q. What differences did you record between existing and desired practice?

Q. What is the average 'participation' score for 'existing' and 'desired' participation for each section?

Q. Read the companion paper about the development of the diagnostic tool. Calculate the democracy index for your responses (and - if you come from the same organisation – for the group as a whole).

Q. Based on the definition of 'workplace democracy' in the companion paper, **is your workplace democratic?**

To learn how this diagnostic tool was developed, and how to apply it during action learning / action research, see the following paper.

Ridley-Duff, R. and Ponton, A. (2013) 'Workforce participation: developing a theoretical framework for a longitudinal study', *Journal of Co-operative Studies*, 46(3): 3-23, http://shura.shu.ac.uk/7442/

Additional support documentation is available on the FairShares Wiki.

Activity 2.7 – Advanced governance diagnostics

This survey presents six groups of five questions - a full set of Advanced Governance Diagnostics.

The questions build on the initial governance audit that you may have completed earlier. This time the survey explores the ideology that underpins governance practices with each stakeholder in an enterprise of your choice. Of all the diagnostics, this is the most comprehensive - it can take as long as 30 - 45 minutes to complete. As it is much longer, the paper versions are not reproduced in this book. You can download two PDF documents from the following website: the first contains the questionnaire; the second contains information on how to interpret the results.

www.fairshares.coop/advanced-governance-diagnostics

The questionnaire is a learning tool, not a test. It contributes by:
- Promoting self-awareness of the responsibilities accepted by board members
- Promoting self-awareness of the way authority and control affects your organisational role.

There are no right or wrong answers. The diagnostic nature of the tool does not test for levels of compliance with legal codes, codes of governance or conduct. Nor does it evaluate your performance individually, or your board's performance as a whole. Instead, it helps you develop a deep understanding of the ideology that informs decision-making and problem-solving in your organisational role so that you can reassess its effectiveness.

There are six sections divided into two groups. The first is **External Relations**:

- Regulators and Regulation
- Stakeholder Management
- Funders and Investors

The second is **Internal Relations:**

- Employees, Members and Volunteers
- Executives and Management
- Board Development and Maintenance

In each section, there will be six questions: four ask you to describe how decisions are made on a topic, then a fifth asks you how you would like to make similar decisions in the future. Each section focuses on your relationship with a stakeholder group and contains questions on: a) decision-making; b) risk/opportunity management; c) dispute resolution, and d) communications.

In all cases, choose answers that most closely match your perception of how the organisation would respond at the moment, and then (at the end of each section) state your personal preference for the future.

Distance Learning: You can complete the Advanced Governance Diagnostics **online:**

www.fairshares.coop/advanced-governance-diagnostics/

Use the Learning and Teaching version.

To learn about the underlying theories that inform this diagnostic tool, see the following papers.

Ridley-Duff, R. (2007) 'Communitarian perspectives on social enterprise', *Corporate Governance: An International Review*, 15(2): 382-92, http://shura.shu.ac.uk/721/.

Chadwick-Coule, T (2011). Social dynamics and the strategy process: bridging or creating a divide between trustees and staff? *Non-profit and Voluntary Sector Quarterly*, **40** (1): 33-56, http://shura.shu.ac.uk/5576/.

Additional support documentation is available on the FairShares Wiki.

Activity 2.8 - Reviewing governance diagnostics

Pre-work - Activities 2.4 and 2.8

In 2014, the FairShares Association created an online version of a Governance Diagnostic Questionnaire included in the first edition of *Understanding Social Enterprise: Theory and Practice*. For the second edition, the questions were revised to cover principles of responsible management such as sustainability, ethics and stakeholder representation. The diagnostic retains the same underlying meta-theoretical assumptions (see Activity 2.4).

Governance systems are seen as something that emerge dynamically from the responses of stakeholders who have power and which either include or exclude 'other' stakeholders. The diagnostics enable students to scrutinise (and reflect) on which orientations are dominant in an organisation, industrial sector or organisation type.

The diagnostics are designed primarily for people who interact with governing bodies (elected members, executives, secretariats, directors). It can also be used as a capacity building tool for future governors.

Now you have discussed the nature of governance and used the Advanced Governance Diagnostics, debate the following questions in an assignment or class discussion.

Questions

1. Which *stakeholders* do you recognise for governance?
2. What issues are raised with each stakeholder group that participates in governance?
3. How do you work with stakeholders who are not recognised?
4. Can you determine any patterns in the responses you have given (or studied) (i.e. preferences for individual or collective decision-making, unitary or pluralist controls)?

Activity 2.9 - Using FairShares to end exploitation

Define the term 'primary stakeholders' for the purpose of this discussion so that students are aware of the interests of:

1. social entrepreneurs (founders)
2. producers and employees (labour)
3. customers and service users (users)
4. social and community investors (investors).

Read the short article The Case for FairShares on the FairShares Association website (www.fairshares.coop/the-case-for-fairshares) then answer the following questions.

1. In the private and voluntary sectors, how is power and wealth *accumulated* by managers and owners?
2. How can enterprises be redesigned so that power and wealth is *distributed* to primary stakeholders?
3. Apply the *FairShares Model* to an enterprise of your choice: what aspects of its ownership, governance and management would need to change before it could claim alignment with the *FairShares Model*? (See Appendix A).

Introduce students to the FairShares Model Enterprise (Example) to learn about designing enterprises. The URL is:

> https://www.loomio.org/g/ugICXanW/fairshares-model-enterprise-an-example

[cc] BY-NC-SA   Rory Ridley-Duff, Mike Bull and FairShares Association, 2015, Creative Commons 4.0, Attribution, Non-Commercial, ShareAlike. Non-exclusive commercial rights granted to Sage Publications.

Activity 2.10 - Combatting wealth inequality

Watch the following video based on data from a Harvard University study by Norton and Ariely (discussed in Part 1 of this book).

https://www.youtube.com/watch?v=QPKKQnijnsM

In small groups, read New Co-operativism and the FairShares Model then discuss the following two questions:

(Download from: www.fairshares.coop/what-is-fairshares/fairshares-and-new-cooperativism)

1. How does the constitution of an enterprise control the distribution of wealth created by its workforce?
2. What rules can you add to a constitution to ensure that a different (more 'ideal') distribution is achieved?

(cc) BY-NC-SA

Rory Ridley-Duff, Mike Bull and FairShares Association, 2015, Creative Commons 4.0, Attribution, Non-Commercial, ShareAlike.

Non-exclusive commercial rights granted to Sage Publications.

Activity 2.11 – Role play: taking big decisions

Future Energy Ltd, a specialist in renewable energy production, has been involved in a government funded venture/collaboration with a network of community groups in deprived urban areas to promote the use of renewable energy in housing association accommodation. The project was successful and you are now considering the commercial viability of continuing the project.

Future Energy Ltd

Future Energy has developed self-build renewable community energy technology. Now the project has completed, a *housing association* would like to contribute roof space (on blocks of flats and semi-detached homes) and internal infrastructure (piping and plumbing etc.). This would provide sites to implement the new solar panel technology created by Future Energy Ltd. There are *community groups* who want to contribute labour to install the self-build systems in housing association properties.

You are a member of Future Energy Ltd, which is structured as a FairShares Company. You are being asked by the housing association and community groups to supply panels and share engineering skills to make the panels efficient. They are proposing that all partners contribute time and technology without making 'up-front' charges, and that Feed-In Tariff payments will be shared when energy is generated.[155]

Estimated Benefits, Profits and Surplus

A consultant has worked out that a household participating in a scheme will – on average – save £100/year in energy costs and generate a payment of £250/year. The first £170 is for generating electricity, and the other £80 is for exporting surplus energy to the national grid.

The housing association in this project has 20,000 properties, but only 7,500 are 'south facing' and fully suitable for installation. A further 2,500 might be suitable if the housing association does some work before installation work begins. This means that the scheme can save *at least* £750,000 a year in energy costs for residents, and generate *at least* £1.85m of additional revenue to be divided equally between the housing association and Future Energy.

Future Energy would normally charge £5,000 per installation, but after training community members in the self-build technology, it estimates the cost will drop to an

---

[155] Gov.uk, 'Feed In Tariffs', https://www.gov.uk/feed-in-tariffs;
Energy Saving Trust, 'Solar Energy Calculator',
http://www.pvfitcalculator.energysavingtrust.org.uk/

average of £2,000 per installation (for the solar panels themselves and transportation costs). Currently, the cost of producing solar panels is falling at about 30% every 5 years.

The consultant estimates that each household will generate an average 3000kWh of energy, cut CO^2 production by 33 tonnes and earn £7,000 in revenues over its lifespan (20 years). Of this amount, £2,000 goes to the household in energy cost savings. This leaves £5,000 to be split between the housing association and Future Energy Ltd. The total earnings (based on 7,500 homes) would be a half share of £37.5m (£18.25m).

However, Future Energy Ltd would spend £15m in materials and transport costs so the nett return is between £3.5m (7,500 homes) and £4.38m (10,000 homes). As a FairShares Company, the first 30% of surplus (£1.05m) is allocated to reserves. The rest is split between Investors (30%), Employees (35%) and Users (35%). Over the life of the project this would generate:

1. Between £0.74m and £1m in earnings for Investor Shareholders (30% share of nett surplus).
2. Between £0.86m and £1.17m for both Labour and User Shareholder (35% share of nett surplus).

The proposal to members of Future Energy Ltd

A scheme has been proposed in which Future Energy Ltd licenses its technology for this and *other community groups and housing associations* to use on a non-commercial basis (i.e. they are not allowed to sell the technology or anything based on it without Future Energy's permission).

You have to decide whether to support the proposal.

You will be allocated to one of the four shareholder groups. Discuss the proposals with other members of your group and decide how to vote.

You vote as an individual, not as a group, and you are also free to refine the proposal, or suggest a different proposal.

*Future Energy Ltd is a FairShares Company with Founders, Employees (Labour), Customers (Users) and Investors who each hold shares and have voting power that is exercised in a General Assembly. Normally votes are taken on a simple one-member, one-vote basis, but there are provisions in the constitution for a Special Resolution that must be passed by majority vote in **every** stakeholder group.*

Guidance to shareholders

Founders

You are one of a number of founders of Future Energy Ltd (from a group of scientists) who have created a renewable energy company based on your research. Although you want some return for your efforts, your principal motivation is to provide as many people as possible with low cost / free energy.

Employees

You are one of the employees of Future Energy Ltd, a renewable energy company. After 1 year of service, you became a member-owner entitled to a share of annual profits. Although you are sympathetic to the pursuit of sustainable development, your principal interest is to advance your career as an engineer / technician / manager in the field of renewable energy, and ensure a good lifestyle for your family.

Customers

You are one of the customers of Future Energy Ltd. When you bought their solar panels, you became a member-owner and now obtain income from the electricity you generate for the company. Although you are sympathetic to the idea of sustainable development, your principal reason for becoming a member is to get free energy.

Investors

You are one of a number of investors in Future Energy Ltd, a renewable energy company created using the Founders research. Although you are sympathetic to the idea of sustainable development, your principal reason for investing is to get a reasonable financial return (over 5% per annum).

Activity details

1. Divide the study group into four sub-groups: Founders, Employees (Labour), Customers (Users) and Investors.
2. Send out the briefing materials (above) in advance of the session (or ask students to get the book on Kindle and read this activity).
3. Convene the groups and conduct a debate for up to 15 minutes on whether to support the proposal. Remind each person that they will vote as an individual, not as a group.
4. Issue slips of paper for the members of each group to cast their votes (remembering to note on each slip which type of shareholder it has been issued to).
5. After 15 minutes, chair the voting process (follow Clauses 21 to 26 in the FairShares Model Company Rules in Part 3 of the book).
6. **If voting is by *simple majority*,** will the proposal pass? (It will pass if more than half the group vote for the proposal).
7. **If a *poll* is called,** will the proposal pass? (Weighted voting applies – see how to adjust the votes in Clause 24).
8. **If a *special resolution* is called**, will the proposal pass? (It will pass if a majority in every sub-group votes for the proposal, and 75% of voters are in favour).

Distance learning guidance

1. You can vote on an ordinary resolution vote online using the FairShares Model Enterprise (on Loomio) (if you are not

reading this as an eBook, search Google for "FairShares Model Enterprise" or enter the URL: https://www.loomio.org/g/ugICXanW/fairshares-model-enterprise-example).

2. Join the General Assembly (create an account if you need to).
3. Invite all your students into the General Assembly.
4. Open the 'Students' group and ask to join as a 'Co-ordinator' (a member of the FairShares Association can give you permission to invite your students into the Students group).
5. Invite all your students into the Students group (do this after inviting them into the General Assembly). Students will need to accept their invitations and (if necessary) create a Loomio account *before* they can vote.[156]
6. Send the activity materials to the students (or ask them to get this book on Kindle/Kobo and read Activity 2.11).
7. Loomio already has (summary) material on the Future Energy Ltd proposal in each sub-group.
8. Add a proposal to the Students group (remember to include the class/institution name in the discussion title).[157]
9. Set a proposal deadline so that it coincides with the end of the lecture (or lecture series, if you want to give students more time to investigate the project options).
10. Loomio will automatically remind students to vote on your proposal 24 hours before the deadline you set.
11. After the vote, announce the result on Loomio (every student will get notified).

[cc] BY-NC-SA

Maureen McCulloch and Rory Ridley-Duff, 2015, Creative Commons 4.0, Attribution, Non-Commercial, ShareAlike.

---

[156] To make this simpler, Loomio permits signing in with Facebook, Google or Persona.
[157] Loomio's 'Create Proposal' command enables group members to vote on a proposal. Propose that the consultant's proposal be accepted.

Activity 2.12 - Building a solidarity enterprise

(Practitioner / Consultant Project Task)

Watch this video (*Shift Change*) to get a feel for solidarity at work:

http://vimeo.com/38342677

Imagine that you are planning to establish a new solidarity enterprise that will source fair trade goods and then supply them to cafés, universities, housing groups, public authorities, schools and private companies in a city/region.

You have been tasked with designing an enterprise that will incorporate *FairShares Model* principles. Information about the antecedent models that led to FairShares have been circulated to your team.

1. Divide the class into groups of four students. Allocate each group member **one** antecedent case to study (from Cases 7.1, 7.2, 7.3, 7.4)

Download 'recent cases' from:

http://www.fairshares.coop/what-is-fairshares/fairshares-and-new-co-operativism/

If undertaking as a project, study the model rules in Part 3 of this book to generate further debate and discussion.

1. Ask team members to study one antecedent model each to establish its contribution to the *FairShares Model*.
2. Ask team members to share their findings on the merits (or not) of each antecedent model.
3. Establish your own *FairShares Model* adapted to serve the needs of your new enterprise.
4. Ask each team to present the *values and principles* that they have agreed, and which they will apply to their new social enterprise.

There is a FairShares Model Enterprise on Loomio as a study aid for students. The full URL is:

> https://www.loomio.org/g/ugICXanW/fairshares-model-enterprise-an-example

(It may be quicker to Google 'Loomio FairShares Model Enterprise')

You could undertake this as a group project throughout a course. Get each student group to implement their enterprise governance system as a new Loomio Group, invite other students to join it so they can examine and critique it. You can set an assignment task in which students compare different implementations of a solidarity enterprise (using their Loomio Groups as the empirical evidence of their ideas).

(cc) BY-NC-SA

Rory Ridley-Duff, Mike Bull and FairShares Association, 2015, Creative Commons 4.0, Attribution, Non-Commercial, ShareAlike.

Non-exclusive commercial rights granted to Sage Publications.

Activity 2.13 - Building a FairShares curriculum

(Educator / Research Project Task)

The following documentation has been created as part of a project to compare course curricula for teaching *Principles of Responsible Management.* The overall project takes five different approaches - social enterprise, cooperative enterprise, responsible management education, Balance (Mike Bull) and FairShares (Rory Ridley-Duff).

In each case, the guiding principles (competencies) of the approach were identified. This appears in the first column. The second and third columns contain the knowledge and skills needed to become competent. The frameworks provide a guide to educators who need to create course, module and seminar learning outcomes.

On the pages that follow is a draft curriculum for developing a FairShares course. In future editions of this book, a final curriculum will be published. This activity involves developing the framework by identifying the personal qualities, academic papers / texts, and learning activities that can deliver the curriculum. The core competencies are identified as the ability:

1. To define social purpose(s)
2. To create and assess the social impact(s) of trading
3. To practice ethical production
4. To practice ethical consumption
5. To design socialised (member-)ownership systems
6. To design socialised (member-driven) governance and management system

For this project, add three new columns:

- Behaviours (to behave with…)
- Academic support (articles / books)
- Learning activities (course elements)

Fill them in to design your FairShares course.

Competence (FairShares Principle)	Knowledge (to know…)	Skills (Know How): (to be able to…)
A. To define social purpose(s)	- The nature of values and belief systems - The nature of, and approaches to, social entrepreneurship - The difference between a person and purpose-centred strategy - Processes for setting (collective) goals - How to participate in setting social targets - Values-based marketing	Investigate and evaluate the value systems of individuals, organisations and institutions to establish their orientation towards economic, social and environmental value creation.
		Distinguish responsible, mutual and charitable modes of trading, and review social enterprise approaches based on a mix of redistribution, reciprocity and market exchange.
		Differentiate 'socialised enterprises' and 'social purpose enterprises' from each other and from private and public enterprises.
		Initiate, organise, facilitate and finalise a deliberative process that reaches well-articulated policy outcomes and decisions that command a high level of social support.

Educating for Change

Competence (FairShares Principle)	Knowledge (to know...)	Skills (Know How): (to be able to...)
		Satisfy human needs by creating products and services that improve social / environmental outcomes without depleting or destroying human, social, ethical, intellectual and natural capital.
		Evaluate the relative importance of processes and purposes in the context of developing a social enterprise plan.
B. To create and assess the social impact(s) of trading	• Theories of social innovation • Processes for social value creation and tracking • SROI (social returns) and Social / Environmental Auditing • Processes for preparing social / environmental accounts (integrated accounting) • How to interpret social / integrated accounts • Sustainable supply chain development	Describe and explain different types of social value, different approaches to social value creation and sustainable development.
		Devise social enterprise strategies / plans that review and audit assumptions about social value creation, social and/or environmental impacts.
		Distinguish technical innovation from social innovation and establish how technical innovations can support social innovation.
		Contribute to the preparation and review of verbal and written social and environmental reports and/or accounting procedures.
		Participate in the preparation and review of a social / environmental audit.
		Compare and contrast social return on investment (SROI) with social accounting and auditing (SAA).
C. To practice ethical production	• Ethics and (social) entrepreneurship • Sustainable development • Environmental management (up to point of sale) • Non-linear sustainable supply chain management • Human relations management / development (HRM) • Member relations management / development (MRM)	Engage in (or support) social entrepreneurs as they make ethical choices in enterprise development.
		Integrate sustainable development issues into production processes and supply chain development.
		Manage the environmental impacts of a production system.
		Improve the quality of human relations between producers through inclusive human relationship management systems.
		Manage producer / member relationships through inclusive processes for decision-making, communication and dispute resolution.

Competence (FairShares Principle)	Knowledge (to know...)	Skills (Know How): (to be able to...)
	• Employment / industrial relations (ER / IR) • Worker and member participation • The ethics of institutional and crowd funding • Fair trade production	Manage relations between those who employ others and are employed by others to ensure that they jointly negotiate the rules and procedures needed for sustainable production.
		Devise systems to share information on the outcomes of worker / member participation in production.
		Critically compare institutional and crowd-funding strategies and evaluate their impact on social / environmental value creation. Assess how an enterprise can support or integrate fair trade principles into its production.
D. To practice ethical consumption	• Sustainable consumption • Circular economy • Business models for sustainability • Ethical selling / retailing • Customer / client relations • Fair trade consumption	Integrate sustainable development principles into marketing, selling and distribution.
		Prioritise the marketing of goods / services that contribute to human well-being and sustainability.
		Regulate the selling of goods and services through the concept of 'sufficiency' rather than 'profit maximisation'.
		Respond to client / customer concerns and complaints.
		Where possible, prioritise purchases that make recycling more possible / practical
		Reduce the consumption needed for production (without reducing quality).
		Where possible/practical, preferentially purchase fair trade goods.
E. To design socialised (member-) ownership systems	• The nature of solidarity, mutuality and cooperative behaviour • Primary, secondary and tertiary stakeholders • Models for member-control and ownership • The nature and impact of incorporation • The impact of incorporation on	Engage members in the study of group ownership, and its links to solidarity and mutual principles.
		Distinguish primary, secondary and tertiary stakeholders for a proposed or existing enterprise.
		Craft rules (Articles of Association) to support maximisation of ownership and control by a social enterprise's primary stakeholders.
		Differentiate share characteristics in private, social and cooperative businesses to select the 'best fit' or 'best mix' for a new venture.

Educating for Change

Competence (FairShares Principle)	Knowledge (to know...)	Skills (Know How): (to be able to...)
	governance and management	Promote an ownership solution to a community of people (geographical or virtual) using both traditional and digital communication techniques.
		Critically assess the likely impact of incorporating a legal entity on individuals, groups and corporate members.
		Actively reflect on the linkages between ownership systems, relations of production and environmental outcomes.
F. To design socialised (member-driven) governance and management	• Civil society and industrial democracy • Participatory economics and management • Communitarian governance • Employee / member involvement and participation • Social and environmental accounting and auditing	Critically assess the inter-sections between (and the impacts of) civil society and industrial democracy on production and consumption.
		Critically engage and compare the assumptions of 'participatory' and 'free market' approaches to economics and management.
		Differentiate communitarian (collective) and liberal (individualistic) governance practices and assess their impact on primary stakeholders.
		Participate in the creation of systems that enable employees / members to manage their involvement and participation in management.
		Articulate experiences – and collect and collate secondary sources of information - to assess how production and consumption is impacting on people and the environment.

That's it for Part 2. In Part 3, I set out updated model rules for companies, cooperatives and associations. These have been changed to accommodate the use of Web 2.0 technologies in governance and management. Designed with the internet age in mind, FairShares V2.1 Model Rules provide for online meetings, social networking and collaborative decision-making.

Whilst I appreciate that educational materials (Part 2) and model rules (Part 3) will be read by fewer people than Part 1, in this book (particularly in its eBook format) they form part of an interactive intellectual commons. Each activity contains pointers to materials on the FairShares website and links to documentation in the FairShares Wiki. I hope this interactive, user-driven experience, helps you engage with the education materials and model rules. I also hope your proficiency in using them will eventually exceed mine so that you take control of their development.

Part 3 – Instituting Change

In Part 3, I provide a copy of the model rules in FairShares V2.1 to catalyse the creation of FairShares companies, cooperatives and associations. You will need to translate / adapt these to fit your legal and culture context. Where possible the FairShares Association can put you in touch with a business adviser and/or FairShares expert.

- *Model Rules for a FairShares Company* – this offers a model for registering under the applicable law for a joint-stock company in your jurisdiction and is designed to issue non-tradable par-value shares to Founders, Labour and Users for membership and governance, and tradable variable yield (ordinary) Investors Shares to represent wealth created. In a FairShares company, Investors Shares are (by default) traded only amongst Founder, Labour and User members and mutual/social enterprises created for employee, community and public benefit (including other FairShares enterprises). Moreover, the manner in which they are traded ensures that shares contribute to mutual, not private, control of the enterprise (private transfers of shares are not permitted).

- *Model Rules for a FairShares Cooperative* – this is for registering under the applicable cooperative / society law for the jurisdiction. It is designed to issue non-tradable par-value shares to Founders, Labour and Users. Additional (par value) Investor Shares are issued to represent each member's share of the wealth created. Unlike a FairShares company, shares are withdrawable (at face value) and are not tradable. They can, however, be gifted to approved mutual social enterprises created for employee, community and public benefit (including other FairShares enterprises).

- *Model Rules for a FairShares Association* – this can be used for unincorporated and incorporated associations in the relevant jurisdiction. A FairShares Association has members, but no owners. The provisions for governance are similar to a FairShares company and cooperative, but surpluses can only be allocated to projects that meet the aims of the association. They cannot be distributed for private benefit. It is, therefore, suitable for the creation of non-profit associations that protect assets for a specific purpose or community.

FairShares Model rules contain clauses that enable you to brand yourself as a solidarity enterprise, a worker-controlled enterprise or a user-controlled enterprise (Figure 3.1).

Figure 3.1 – Identities for FairShares Enterprises

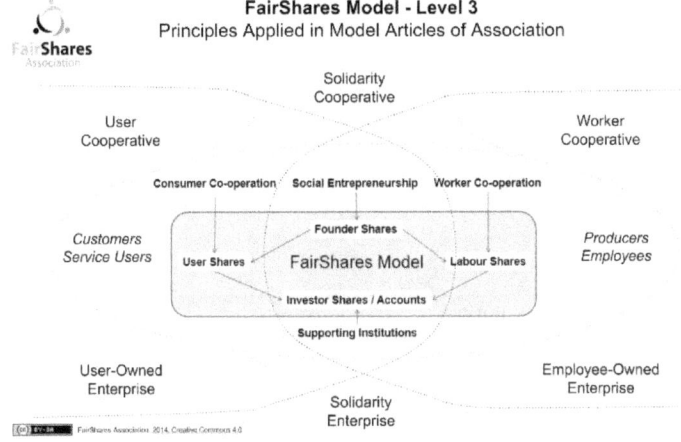

Copyright 2015, Rory Ridley-Duff,
Creative Commons 4.0 Licence, BY-NC-SA

In Table 3.1, each set of model rules are mapped against the characteristics set out in activities 2.1 and 2.5.[158]

---

[158] Based on Ridley-Duff, R. and Southcombe, C. (2012) "The Social Enterprise Mark: a critical review of its conceptual dimensions", *Social Enterprise Journal*, 8(3): 178-200, Table IV,

Instituting Change

Look at the findings of your Social Enterprise Survey and Advanced Management Diagnostics. Choose the model rules that meet your identity needs: association rules can accommodate philanthropy while cooperative and company versions are oriented toward mutuals and cooperatives.

Table 3.1 – Mutual / Responsible / Charitable Trading

	FairShares Model		
Mutual Trading (Cooperative Business)	Coop	Company	Association
• Co-owned by one or more of its primary stakeholders	Yes	Yes	No
• Offers membership to primary stakeholders	Yes	Yes	Yes
• Ensures that most (or all) of its assets are used for member, community and public benefit	All three	All three	Community and Public
• Governed by one or more of its primary stakeholders	Yes	Yes	Yes
• Continuously encourages cooperative working / networking	Yes	Yes	Yes
• Allows members to equitably contribute to, and receive distributions of, capital/surpluses	Yes	Yes	Contribute only
• Provides technical and political education/training to its members	Yes	Yes	Yes
Responsible Trading (Social Business)	Coop	Company	Association
• Not controlled by private / public sectors.	Yes	Yes	Yes
• States (and reviews) its ethical values and principles	Social Audit included	Social Audit Included	Social Audit Included
• Provides at least some paid employment	Trading is an objective	Trading is an objective	Trading is an objective
• Provides evidence that it makes a positive social impact and/or runs for community benefit	Social audit and mutual principles	Social audit and mutual principles	Social audit and mutual principles
• Educates the public about the benefits of its business model	Yes	Yes	Yes
• Receives most of its income from trading activities, not grants or donations	Member determined	Member determined	Member determined

Charitable Trading (Philanthropic)	Coop	Company	Association
• Continuously produces and/or sells goods and services to improve well-being	Specified object	Specified object	Specified object
• Reinvests most of its surplus/profit back into its social/environmental purpose	70 – 100%	70 – 100%	100%
• Makes clear statements about its social and/or environmental purposes/objectives	Yes	Yes	Yes
• Balances member (stakeholder) needs with sustainable development goals	Yes	Yes	More on sustainability
• Discourages a 'for-profit' mind-set	Partial	Partial	Yes
• Based on the actions of citizens voluntarily working together	Yes	Yes	Yes
• Has members/founders who bear a significant level of risk	Yes	Yes	Maybe

Model rules version 2.1, 1st July 2015

Model rules are licensed to the FairShares Association under a Creative Commons Licence by Rory Ridley-Duff and Cliff Southcombe.

> All model rules are provided 'as is' under a Creative Commons Licence. They can be shared and adapted for your own use, providing the copyright of the association is acknowledged (as shown below) and new versions are made available under the same Creative Commons Licence.

© FairShares Association, 2015
Creative Commons 4.0: Attribution,
Non-Commercial Share Alike

> No warranty is provided that they are suitable for your situation. They are provided to stimulate and inform innovation in cooperative and social enterprise development, to inform practice, and also to stimulate new thinking about the democratisation of management, ownership and governance in a socially enterprising economy.
>
> As with all model rules, professional advice is recommended to help you adapt them to your specific needs and circumstances.

Instituting Change

Model Rules for a FairShares Company

[COMPANIES ACT]
Company Limited by Shares

Articles of Association for
[COMPANY NAME]

Clause	Article Text
1	**Definitions.** In these Articles:-
	"the Act" means the [Companies Act] and any amendments in force, including those enacted in the [Subsequent Companies Act Revisions].
	"Cash" includes cheques, electronic fund transfers, IOUs, promissory notes and money orders.
	"Member" a holder of a Labour, User, Investor or Founder Share.
	"Beneficiary" a service user, member holding only Investor Shares, or organisation listed in Clause 54 as a beneficiary of the community dividend.
	"Qualifying Contribution" means a commitment to trade with the Company in a way that meets the criteria for membership. Qualifying contributions are set for Labour Shareholders and User Shareholders only.
	"Quorum" a meeting in which a sufficient number of people are present to take decisions.
	"Ordinary Resolution" means a proposal accepted by a majority of votes cast on a one-shareholder, one-vote basis, irrespective of shareholder class, subject to any adjustments provided for in Clause 23 and 24 of these rules.
	"Class Resolution" means a proposal accepted by a majority of votes cast in one shareholder class on a one-shareholder one-vote basis.
	"Special Resolution" means a proposal accepted by a majority of votes cast in each shareholder class separately, on a one-shareholder one-vote basis, plus at least [75%] of all members irrespective of shareholder class on a one-shareholder one-vote basis.
	"Reserves" exclude the current year's profit and loss account.

Clause	Article Text
	"Labour Shares" are shares owned by a member who makes qualifying labour contributions in the Company, entitling her or him to participate in Company governance and receive a share of surplus. For the purposes of clarity, any person recognised in UK Employment law as a 'worker' will qualify for Labour Shares if they make a qualifying contribution.
	"User Shares" are shares owned by a member who makes a qualifying contribution through their trading or usage of the Company's products / services, entitling her or him to participate in Company governance and receive a share of surplus. For the purposes of clarity, any person recognised as a beneficiary or a customer of the organisation will qualify for User Shares if they make a qualifying contribution.
	"Investor Shares" are shares owned by a member who invests unremunerated labour or equity capital entitling him or her to a share of the Company's assets and surplus.
	"Founder Shares" are shares owned by a Company founder, entitling them to govern the company.
	"IPS" is a former Industrial and Provident Society, now a Cooperative Society
	"CIC" is a Community Interest Company.
2	Regulations in [Companies Act] do not apply unless they are referenced directly in these rules.
3	The name of the Company is [COMPANY NAME].
4	The registered office of the Company is in [Territory].
5	The Company's objects are:
	a. to engage in commerce and social activities that spreads wealth and power amongst the Company's primary stakeholders (producers, employees, customers and service users);
	b. to pursue trading activities that are economically, socially and environmentally sustainable, and which improve the well-being of the Company's primary stakeholders;
	c. to promote the development of social entrepreneurship;
	d. to advance Cooperative Values and Principles that create social capital through participatory management and democratic governance processes;
	e. to abide by the internationally recognised values and principles of cooperative identity as defined by the International Cooperative Alliance (ICA), in particular the values of self-help, self-responsibility, democracy, equality and solidarity and the ethical values of honesty, openness, social responsibility and caring for others;

Instituting Change

Clause	Article Text
	f. to abide by principles of equality of opportunity and oppose forms of discrimination on the grounds of social class, race, ethnic origin, gender, sexual preference, age, disability and religion;
	g. [Add other social / community / public benefit objectives here].
6	The liability of members is limited.
7	The Company has the power to do anything which is conducive to the furtherance of its objects subject to constraints specified in these Articles of Association.
8	The Company's initial share capital is [£1]:
	a. [1] Founder Share(s) of nominal value £1.
9	These rules may be altered only by Special Resolution of all shareholder classes, i.e. passed by a majority of votes cast in each shareholder class separately and an overall [75%] of members in favour, on a one-shareholder, one-vote basis.

MEMBERSHIP, CAPITAL AND FAIRSHARES BRANDING	
Clause	Article Text
10	**Membership and Share Capital:** The Company is open to applications for membership in the appropriate class without discrimination, subject to making a qualifying contribution agreed by members in General Meeting. A list of qualifying contributions will be made available to current and prospective members, and will specify: the conditions under which a Labour and/or User share will be issued; the transactions with the Company that qualify an applicant for membership in each class: • If there are qualifying contributions for both Labour and User Shares, the Company may be branded as a FairShares Solidarity Enterprise. • If there are qualifying contributions for User Shares, but no qualifying contributions for Labour Shares, the Company may be branded as a FairShares User-Owned Enterprise. • If there are qualifying contributions for Labour Shares, but no qualifying contributions for User Shares, the Company may be branded as a FairShares Employee-Owned Enterprise. • If there are no qualifying contributions for either User or Labour Shares, the Company is not a FairShares Company / Social Enterprise, and shall not be entitled to use FairShares Branding, or call itself a FairShares Company / Social Enterprise. a. The rights and conditions attaching to shares are:

Clause		Article Text
	i.	Founder Shares: issued at a £1 par value to the natural or legal persons who found the enterprise; non-transferable; one vote per shareholder at General Meetings (except as defined in Clauses 23 and 24); 1p fixed preference dividend; forfeited on holder's death, bankruptcy or insolvency; cancelled without payment on winding up.
	ii.	Labour Shares: issued at par value to natural or legal persons who make at least one qualifying contribution in respect of labour provided to the cooperative; issued in proportion to their labour contribution; non-transferable; one vote per shareholder at General Meetings; forfeited on holder's death, bankruptcy or insolvency; cancelled upon cessation of contracts pertaining to their labour contribution; cancelled without payment on winding up.
	iii.	User Shares: issued at par value to natural or legal persons who make a qualifying contribution in the use of the cooperative's products and services; non-transferable; one vote per shareholder at General Meetings; forfeited on holder's death, bankruptcy or insolvency; cancelled upon the cessation of a trading relationship; cancelled without payment on winding up.
	iv.	Investor Shares: issued to any natural or legal person; issued at the Fair Price to investors of equity capital upon payment; issued as 'Member Shares' to providers of labour in proportion to the Capital Gain created by their labour; issued as 'Member Shares' to customers / service users in proportion to the Capital Gain created by their trading activity; one vote per shareholder in General Meeting; transferable after [3] years or termination of membership or retirement or death (with compensation at the Fair Price) to one of the following:
		1. A FairShares Labour Association, Employee Benefit Trust or other Cooperative Society established for the purpose of buying and selling (redeeming) Labour shareholders' investor shares and managing them for the benefit of the Company's employees;
		2. A FairShares Solidarity Association, Charitable Trust, Charitable Company or Charitable Incorporated Organisation established for the purpose of buying and selling (redeeming) members' investor shares and managing them for public benefit;
		3. A FairShares User Association, Community Interest Company, Community Benefit Society, FairShares

Instituting Change

Clause		Article Text
		Company or FairShares Cooperative created or selected to purchase (redeem) members' investor shares and manage them for community benefit.
	v.	For the avoidance of doubt, upon death, a member's Founder, User and Labour shares are cancelled without payment, and the member's Investor Shares will be transferred to other members or organisations established in accordance with Clause 10(a)(iv) with compensation at the Fair Price, then paid into their estate for the benefit of their next of kin. A member's next of kin may not inherit Investor Shares.
	vi.	For the avoidance of doubt, each member has only one vote at General Meetings, irrespective of the number of shares and number of share classes held.
	b.	**Alteration of Share Capital.** The Company may issue only new Labour, User or Investor Shares.
11.		**Transfer of Investor Shares.**
	a.	Investor Shares may be sold (redeemed) at the Fair Price (see Clause 15) to institutions in accordance with Clause 10 (a) (iv), providing the Investor Shareholder is not in debt to the Company.
	b.	The 5 members who have traded the most Investor Shares over the last 5 years should be listed, together with their contact details, at the start of the register of members.
	c.	Nothing in these articles requires title to securities to be evidenced or transferred by a written instrument if the Act permits otherwise.
12.		**Equity Capital Stakes.**
	a.	Every natural and legal person (director, employee, supplier or self-employed contractor) who makes a qualifying contribution will be offered Labour Shares proportionate to their qualifying contributions at the conclusion of any probationary period agreed by the Company. They will also be offered a chance to purchase Investor Shares to the value of [15%] of their initial labour contract (i.e. a person's annual salary, or projected annual value of the contract for services) after 366 days (1 year + 1 day) of continuous service;
	b.	Every natural and legal person (user, customer) who makes a qualifying contribution will be offered User Shares in proportion to their qualifying contributions. They will also be offered a chance to purchase Investor Shares to the value of [15%] of the value of their product and service purchases from the Company;

Clause		Article Text
	c.	The Company may organise a third-party loan or grant of money for an existing member for the purpose of establishing their Investor Shareholding;
	d.	A contract for labour (director, employee or contractor) may specify that part of the remuneration will be made in the form of Investor Shares;
	e.	After the anniversary of a contract to supply labour (12 months), Investor Shares offered by the Directors can be purchased at the then current Fair Price as defined in 15(b) and 15(c);
	f.	Subject to special resolution, the provisions in clauses 12 (a) to (d) can be applied to other legal entities (companies, cooperatives, associations, charities etc.) who support the work of the Company.
	g.	The Directors shall not be entitled to withhold share offers or prevent share transfers, or reject applications for membership, on the grounds of social class, age, politics, race, creed, religion, culture, ethnic origin, sex or sexual orientation, marital status or disability.
13.		**Valuation.**
	a.	Pre-emption rights are excluded.
	b.	The Company is valued at the start of every financial year, and this is the "Reference Value".
	c.	At incorporation, the Reference Value of the Company is £0.
	d.	Thereafter, the Reference Value shall be calculated as the book value of fixed assets plus 20 (twenty) times the Investor Share for the previous accounting period (see Clause 44).
	e.	A Class Resolution can require revaluation of the Company or any of its assets.
14		**Share Issues.**
	a.	Excluding issues of Member Shares, a "Major Issue" of Investor Shares (increasing issued Investor Shares by more than 50% within 6 months) must be at a share price agreed by ordinary resolution.
	b.	Any other issue of Investor Shares should be at the Fair Price (see 15 (b) and 15 (c)).
15		Capital Gains, Member Shares **and the** Fair Price.
	a.	The **"Capital Gain Fraction"** is 0.5, and may be changed only by special resolution.
	b.	If the Company's value at the end of an accounting period (the **"New Value"**) is greater than its Reference Value, then **Capital Gain** = (New Value − Reference Value) x [Capital Gain Fraction] and:

Instituting Change

Clause		Article Text		
		the "Workers' Gain"	is	Capital Gain / 2;
		the "Users' Gain"	is	Capital Gain / 2;
		the new Fair Price	is	(New Value − Capital Gain) ÷ (Investor Shares Issued);
		the # of Member Shares	is	(Capital Gain) ÷ (new Fair Price);

This number of Member Shares shall be issued as Investor Shares to Labour and User Shareholders by any of the following means:

   i. Issuing Investor Shares to the value of Workers' Gain credited as fully paid to those holding Labour Shares in proportion to the number of Labour Shares held at the commencement of the accounting period;

   ii. Issuing Investor Shares to the value of Users' Gain credited as fully paid to those holding User Shares in proportion to the number of User Shares held at the commencement of the accounting period;

   iii. Purchasing Investor Shares (at the New Fair Price) from existing investor shareholders to the value of Workers' Gain and then issuing them to Labour Shareholders in proportion to the number of Labour Shares held at the commencement of the accounting period, capped at the Workers' Gain;

   iv. Purchasing Investor Shares (at the New Fair Price) from existing investor shareholders to the value of Users' Gain and then issuing them to User Shareholders in proportion to the number of User Shares held at the commencement of the accounting period, capped at the Users' Gain;

   v. Any combination of 15 i) to iv) that has the effect of acquiring for Labour and User Shareholders the number of 'Member Shares' to which they are entitled.

   c. Otherwise, the new Fair Price is (New Value) ÷ (number of Investor Shares in issue).

16 **Borrowing and Investment.**

   a. **Borrowing:** the Board of Directors may exercise all the powers of the Company to borrow money at commercial rates, and to mortgage or charge its undertaking, property and assets (present or future) and to issue debentures provided that:

      i. No borrowing is authorised that exceeds the value of the Reserves unless:

         1. the lender does not take a charge over the assets of the Company;

Clause	Article Text
	2. the loan amount or credit agreement is unsecured (i.e. does not require the Company to offer security);
	3. the borrowing secures for the Company an asset or contract with a value greater than the amount borrowed.
	ii. The borrowing is authorised by an Ordinary Resolution.
	b. **Commercial Investments:** the Board may exercise all the powers of the Company to make commercial investments, provided that the sum invested does not exceed one half of Reserves.
	i. The balance of Reserves must be held in current or deposit accounts, low-risk stocks, bonds or accessible savings accounts.
	c. **Social investments** may be made each year in accordance with Clause 10(iv) providing they total no more than one half of the opening balance of the Redemption Fund for that year.
	GOVERNANCE
17	The Directors may call General Meetings and, on the requisition of members holding a tenth or more of the shares in any class, must convene a General Meeting for a date not later than 4 weeks after receipt of the requisition. General Meetings can take place through an online collaborative decision-making platform using technology agreed by members.
18	In each financial year, a minimum of one General Meeting will be held in addition to the Annual General Meeting (AGM).
	a. No business shall be transacted at a General Meeting unless a quorum of members is present. Unless and until otherwise decided by General Meeting, two-fifths of the membership shall be the quorum, subject to the number of members being more than [10] and less than [50].
	b. In the event of the membership exceeding [50] the quorum shall be [20].
	c. In the event of the membership being less than [10], the quorum shall be one-half.
	d. An invitation to all members to join an online collaborative decision-making platform before a General Meeting shall be sufficient to satisfy the rules regarding a quorum providing all resolutions on which a vote is required are posted to the online collaborative decision-making platform before the meeting.
	e. No business shall be transacted at an off-line General Meeting until the meeting has agreed a chairperson. Online General Meetings will not require a chairperson. Whenever a President

Instituting Change

Clause	Article Text
	is in post, the President will chair an off-line General Meeting. If a President is not in post, or the President is not present, the meeting will elect one of the Trustees to chair the meeting. If no Trustee is present, the meeting may elect a chairperson from those present.
19.	The General Meeting can set corporate policy, approve/reject social enterprise plans, and take decisions about acquisition and disposal of property, and partnership arrangements with other organisations.
	a. A proposal to acquire another organisation may be taken by Ordinary Resolution.
	b. A proposal to merge or sell the Company must be put as a Special Resolution.
	c. A proposal to wind up or dissolve the Company must be put as a Special Resolution.
20	Corporate policy and social enterprise plans are implemented by a Chief Executive Officer or Executive Team appointed by Board Members. The Board will stipulate their authority whenever appointed.
	a. When no Chief Executive Officer or Executive Team is in post, the Board member with the most Labour Shares will assume the responsibilities of the Chief Executive Officer until a new Chief Executive Officer or Executive Team can be appointed.
	b. If the situation in 20(a) arises, and two or more directors have the same number of Labour Shares, the longest serving member will assume the responsibilities of the Chief Executive Officer until a new Chief Executive Officer or Executive Team is appointed.
	c. The Chief Executive Officer or Executive Team is responsible to the General Meeting and Board for the organisation and management of the Company and the implementation of the company's social enterprise plans.
21.	Every Founder, Labour, User and Investor shareholder can attend, speak and propose resolutions at a General Meeting, can stand (subject to clauses 30 and 31) for election as a Director and can cast one vote at General Meetings (except as provided for in clauses 23 and 24).
22.	Any person can act as a proxy for a member at General Meeting. An instrument appointing a proxy must be written in a usual form, or a form approved by the Directors.
	a. A proxy may act for a maximum of one other member at General Meetings (i.e. can cast a maximum of two votes, including their own).
23.	Decisions at off-line General Meetings are made by passing resolutions with a show of hands, unless a poll is demanded by at

Clause	Article Text
	least 2 members. At online General Meetings, decisions are made by approving a member proposal using the collaborative decision-making tools adopted by members.
	a. For Ordinary Resolutions taken by a show of hands (or online vote), Founder, Labour, User and Investor shareholders have one vote each, irrespective of the number of shares held and irrespective of the class(es) of share held.
	b. For Ordinary Resolutions where a poll is called, only Labour Shareholders, User Shareholders and Investor Shareholders vote. Each shareholder votes once, irrespective of the number of shares held. Their vote counts toward each shareholder class in which they hold shares. Founder shareholders vote only if they also hold Labour, User and/or Investor Shares.
	c. If a poll is requested by at least 2 members, the chairperson must offer each shareholder class a chance to pass a Class Resolution in accordance with the provisions of Clause 25 before proceeding with the poll.
24.	On a show of hands, online vote, or poll, every member who is present in person or by proxy, has one vote.
	a. In the event of a poll, the total number of labour, user and investor votes for and against the resolution will be recalculated using the following formulae (see clause 44 for [Investor Share Fraction]; see clause 40 for [Labour Share Fraction] and [User Share Fraction]:
	i. [Investor Votes For] / [Investor Votes Cast] * [Investor Share Fraction]
	ii. [Investor Votes Against] / [Investor Votes Cast] * [Investor Share Fraction]
	iii. [Labour Votes For] / [Labour Votes Cast] * [Labour Share Fraction]
	iv. [Labour Votes Against] / [Labour Votes Cast] * [Labour Share Fraction]
	v. [User Votes For] / [User Votes Cast] * [User Share Fraction]
	vi. [User Votes Against] / [User Votes Cast] * [User Share Fraction]
	b. The total vote for the resolution is the aggregate of i), iii) and v)
	c. The total vote against the resolution is the aggregate of ii), iv) and vi)
	d. For the resolution to pass, the aggregate of i), iii) and v) must be greater than 0.5, otherwise the resolution is not passed.

Instituting Change

Clause	Article Text
	Worked Example – Taking a Poll for an Ordinary Resolution **at a General Meeting**

Investor Votes Cast: 30
Investor Votes For: 18   = 18 / 30 * 30% = 18.0%
Investor Votes Against: 12   = 12 / 30 * 30% = 12.0%
Investor Share Fraction: 30%
Labour Votes Cast: 17
Labour Votes For: 5   = 5 / 17 * 35% = 10.3%
Labour Votes Against: 12   = 12 / 17 * 35% = 24.7%
Labour Share Fraction: 35%
User Votes Cast: 170
User Votes For: 40   = 40 / 170 * 35% = 8.2%
User Votes Against: 130   = 130 / 170 * 35% = 26.8%
User Share Fraction: 35%

Total For = 18% + 10.3% + 8.2% = 36.5%
Total Against = 12% + 24.7% + 26.8% = 63.5%

The resolution is defeated.

25.	A Class Resolution passed by any shareholder class can amend an Ordinary Resolution so that it becomes a Special Resolution (with the exception of contract terminations described in clause 51).

    a. A Special Resolution is passed if:

        i. a majority of votes cast in each shareholder class separately (on a one-shareholder one-vote basis) are in favour of the resolution;

        ii. at least [75%] of all members cast their vote in favour of the resolution, irrespective of shareholder class, on a one-shareholder one-vote basis.

26.	Unless a poll is demanded, a declaration by the chairperson at the meeting that a resolution has, on a show of hands, been carried or lost and an entry to that effect in the book containing the minutes of the proceedings (or equivalent record in an online collaborative decision-making forum) shall be conclusive evidence of the fact without proof of the number or proportions of the votes recorded in favour or against a resolution.
27.	A written resolution signed by all members is valid as if properly passed at a General Meeting.

Clause	Article Text
28.	The proceedings of a meeting are not invalidated by the accidental omission to give notice of the meeting to, or the non-receipt of notice of the meeting by, a person entitled to receive notice.
29.	**Directors**. The Company shall have a Board of between one and [nine] directors except in the circumstances described in clauses 29(a) and (b). A sole director shall have authority to exercise all the powers and authorities vested in the Directors unless:
	a. The company is in receipt of grant or loan funding from a public authority, charitable body or other asset-locked organisation (e.g. a credit union, community cooperative or community interest company), in which case the minimum number of directors shall be three representing at least two shareholder classes, with at least one financial specialist.
	b. The company has [50] or more members, in which case the minimum number of directors shall be five with at least one representing each shareholder class, with at least one financial specialist.
30.	If the Company has fewer than [50] members, directors will be proposed by the Founders or existing Directors and approved by a vote of existing Directors.
	a. Directors may freely negotiate contracts of any value until the Company files its first set of accounts. Thereafter, directors may freely negotiate contracts to the value of [25%] of the company's annual turnover (as reported in the previous year's filed accounts). Contracts in excess of this amount require General Meeting approval.
	b. A Director may be removed at General Meeting by an Ordinary Resolution, or after a vote of no-confidence at a meeting of the Directors.
31.	If the Company has [50] or more members, Directors and a president will be elected annually as follows.
	a. Labour Shareholders will elect a maximum of [two] Directors (one will be subject to re-election by rotation every two-years), following [Companies Act].
	b. User Shareholders will elect a maximum of [two] Directors (one will be subject to re-election by rotation every two-years), following [Companies Act].
	c. Investor Shareholders (if applicable) will elect a maximum of [two] Directors (one will be subject to re-election by rotation every two-years), following [Companies Act].

Instituting Change

Clause		Article Text
	d.	Founder Shareholders will elect a maximum of [two] Directors, who may be removed only by the provisions set out in 31(f).
	e.	A maximum of [one] director may be appointed (co-opted) by the other Directors for their specialist financial skills.
	f.	A director may be removed from office at any General Meeting by a Class Resolution of a shareholder class that elected him or her, or by Ordinary Resolution.
	g.	A Company President will be elected from the Directors on a poll of all shareholders (one vote per shareholder) at the Annual General Meeting. The President has a non-executive role in the running of the Company, and is responsible for overseeing board meetings, maintaining the public image of the Company, and facilitating good communications between Directors and company members. The President has a casting vote at board and General Meetings, but is not required to use it.
	h.	In the absence of a President, or if a President is not elected, the holder(s) of Founder Shares will fulfil this role (as set out in 31(g)).
		i. A Director cannot be removed by other Directors except at General Meeting (as set out in 31 (f)).
		ii. Company Directors may freely negotiate contracts to the value of [12.5%] of the Company's annual turnover (as reported in the previous year's filed accounts). Contracts in excess of this amount require General Meeting approval.
32.		Directors' meetings may be held between General Meetings by any means defined within the Act, and through an online collaborative decision-making platform.
	a.	All acts done by any meeting of the Directors or by any person acting as a member of the Board shall, even if it be afterwards discovered that there was some defect in the appointment of any Board members or person acting as such, or that they or any of them were disqualified, be as valid as if every such person had been duly appointed and was qualified to be a Board member.
		EXPENSES, BENEFITS AND PAY
33.		Providers of labour (Directors, employees, self-employed contractors) shall be paid reasonable expenses wholly incurred in relation to furthering the business of the Company.

Clause		Article Text
	a.	A schedule of acceptable fringe benefits and expenses may be agreed by Ordinary Resolution. Any expenses paid, or fringe benefits provided, outside the scope of an agreed schedule must be itemised in the annual accounts.
	b.	Fringe benefits and expenses must be itemised and recorded in such a way that they can be inspected by any member during normal office hours.
34.		**Remuneration** has three components: Basic Wages ("Pay"), Labour Share dividends and Investor Share dividends.
	a.	Each provider of labour is subject to one or more contracts (employment contract, contract for services or company membership) which controls the manner in which they are remunerated for their labour. These articles, including subsequent modifications, are part of any contract between the Company and those providing labour (Directors, shareholders, employees, self-employed contractors). All members of the company shall be provided with a copy of these rules upon agreement or variation of a contract to supply labour.
	b.	Labour may be recognised solely through Company membership and remunerated solely through Labour Share dividends. A formal contract of employment will be issued if, in the view of the Directors, 'employee status' tests used in employment tribunals have been, or are expected to be, satisfied (i.e. a person works regular hours, receives regular pay, has agreed holiday entitlements and is subject to regular supervision etc.).
	c.	If the Company issues contracts of employment to members of staff, **the maximum ratio between the hourly rate of the highest and lowest paid member of staff shall be [3:1]**. This ratio can only be amended by a Class Resolution in a meeting of Labour Shareholders. This ratio may **not** be amended by Ordinary Resolution or Special Resolution.
	d.	At the start of each accounting period, if the Company has any employees, an amount equal to (Basic Wages × Current Inflation Rate) will be set aside for increases in Basic Wages. The application of any remuneration system to employees and self-employed contractors is at the discretion of the CEO or Executive Team (unless overridden by the procedure set out in clause 49). If the budget for increases in remuneration is not distributed within an accounting period, any unused part **must** be distributed as Investor Shares in proportion to Labour Shareholdings
	e.	An increase in the budget set in 34(d) can only be passed by Special Resolution.

Instituting Change

Clause		Article Text
	f.	Directors' pay and conditions follow the same principles as other Company members and employees.
35.	a.	**"Total Revenue"** means sales plus earnings from services provided plus any other income, but excludes proceeds of new issues of securities or loans obtained
	b.	**"Profit"** is equal to Total Revenue less the cost of materials and services, less depreciation, less rents, less interest.
36.		**"Associated Costs"** means the costs directly associated with a given amount of Pay, including employee's and employer's contributions to insurance schemes, superannuation, healthcare plan, childcare, staff club and any other benefits deducted from pay, together with sickness, maternity, paternity or other statutory pay, and Pay-As-You-Earn income tax.
37.		**"Surplus"** is equal to Profit, less Pay including their Associated Costs, less Corporation Tax.
	a.	The first [£10,000] of Surplus or 30% of Profits (whichever is greater) will be allocated to Reserves as working capital. This amount will be deducted from Surplus before calculating User Share Dividends, Labour Share Dividends and Investor Share Dividends
	b.	Half of the Surplus transferred to reserves will be held in a **"Redemption Fund"**, set aside to fund the creation of organisations defined in Clause 10(a)(iv) that enable members to sell their Investor Shares.
38.		Additional Capital Expenditure, Extraordinary and Research and Development Costs in excess of [£5,000] not financed by an Investor Share Issue must either:
	a.	be deducted from Surplus in exchange for new Investor Shares credited as fully-paid, or
	b.	be paid for from Reserves,
		or as determined by special resolution or a qualified accountant. Any member may ask a qualified accountant to determine if an item comes under these categories.
39.		**"Labour Share"** and **"User Share"**. The Labour and User Share of Surplus, distributed in dividends, is calculated by multiplying [Surplus] (if greater than zero) for the relevant period by the [Labour Share Fraction] and [User Share Fraction]. If [Surplus] is less than or equal to zero, no Labour Share or User Share dividends are paid.

Clause	Article Text
	a. In the event that there are no Labour Shareholders to pay dividends, the Company shall establish or increase a restricted fund to the value of the Labour Share. The Board of Directors may exercise discretion on how to allocate the restricted fund to projects that improve the well-being of the Company's workforce.
	b. In the event that there are no User Shareholders to pay dividends, the Company shall establish or increase a restricted fund to the value of the User Share. The Board of Directors may exercise discretion on how to allocate the restricted fund to projects that improve the well-being of the Company's users.
40.	**"Labour Share Fraction"** and **"User Share Fraction"**
	a. The Labour Share Fraction is [0.35] and User Share Fraction is [0.35] and may be changed only by Special Resolution.
	b. No Labour or User Shareholder may receive a dividend of more than [Surplus] x [Labour Share Fraction].
41.	**"Labour Share Dividends"** and **"User Share Dividends"**
	At the end of an accounting period, the Labour Share and User Share are distributed as dividends to each Labour and User shareholder using the following formulae:
	[Labour Share] x (Member's Labour Shareholding / All Issued Labour Shares). + [User Share] x (Member's User Shareholding / All Issued User Shares)
42.	At the discretion of Directors, all members and employees may be advanced a proportion of their projected Labour Share dividends on a regular basis in addition to monthly Pay. Advances must be listed in the Annual Accounts and deducted from the Labour Share before calculating Labour Share Dividends.
43.	Providers of labour (Directors, employees, self-employed contractors) may, subject to mutual consent, be part-paid by the issue of Investor Shares, credited as fully paid.
44.	Investor Share Interest is paid after Labour and User Share dividends.
	a. The "Investor Share Fraction" is [0.30] and the "Investor Share" is [Surplus] x [Investor Share Fraction]. This may be changed only by special resolution.
	b. The Investor Share Dividend paid in any accounting period is the lowest of the following: i. that which may be paid by law; ii. the [Investor Share] x (1 − [Capital Gain Fraction]); *and*

Clause	Article Text
	iii. the balance of the profit and loss account, if greater than zero;
	c. otherwise it is zero.
	d. The dividend is divided equally between all Investor Shares.
	e. Dividends, if payable, must be paid within [6] calendar months of the end of the accounting period. Interest at the Company's bank overdraft rate is to accumulate on unpaid dividends after this time.
45.	**Shares instead of dividends.** The directors can offer all Investor shareholders the choice of receiving additional Investor Shares credited as fully paid, instead of some or all of the dividend. The directors must specify a procedure fair to all Investor Shareholders for exercising this choice.
46.	No additional sum may be transferred from the profit and loss account to Reserves unless it represents new Investor Shares credited as fully-paid, or is approved by special resolution, or is required by law.
	ACCOUNTING AND AUDITING
47.	Financial and social accounts will be prepared for Board and General Meetings by a person with appropriate bookkeeping and accounting skills / qualifications. They will use accounting conventions agreed by the Board, or as required by the Act. Any member or person authorised in writing by a member may inspect the accounting records during normal working hours.
	a. If the Company has fewer than [50] members, the Board may put an ordinary resolution to the General meeting to approve one of the following:
	I **Either:** the appointment of independent accountants and/or auditors to undertake financial and social audits;
	ii. **Or:** an application for exemption from audit under the provisions of the Act;
	b. If the Company has [50] or more members:
	i. The Board shall recommend a choice of financial and social auditors for approval in General Meeting.
	ii. The selected financial auditor shall audit the company's financial accounts prior to their approval in General Meeting for filing with the relevant regulatory authority.
	iii. The selected social auditor shall assist with audit of the internal democracy and decision-making of the Company, the wages, health and safety, skill sharing and educational opportunities of its members and employees, or other matters concerning the overall personal or job satisfaction of members and employees;

Clause	Article Text
	an assessment of the Company's activities externally, including effects on people, the environment and other organisations.
	iv. An audit committee of up to four people (comprising non-Board members from at least two shareholder classes) will be elected at each AGM.
	v. The purpose of the audit committee is:
	1. to assist and check the preparation of financial records presented to General Meetings so that they are accurate, authentic and meet the needs of members;
	2. to assist and check the preparation of the information needed for a social audit;
	3. to organise elections in accordance with Clause 31;
	4. to record, check and authenticate that the procedures in clauses 17 to 27 are being followed when voting takes place in a General Meeting.
48.	**Accountants, Auditors and Independent Experts.** These must be chosen by ordinary resolution.
	a. The financial auditor (if appointed) shall be from a Recognised Qualifying Body (RQB).
	b. Accountants, Auditors and Independent Experts shall require the accounts to record Members Capital and Community Capital separately.
	i. **"Members' Capital"** is defined as the sum of the value of members' Investor Shareholdings.
	ii. **"Cooperative Capital"** is defined as the sum of grants and donations received from public authorities, charitable bodies and other asset-locked social enterprises (e.g. community benefit societies or community interest companies), plus any capital that members' are required by the Act to convert, or have voluntarily converted, to Cooperative Capital.

DISPUTE RESOLUTION AND INTELLECTUAL PROPERTY	
Clause	Article Text
49.	**Labour Contract Revaluations.** In the event of a dispute, the escalation procedure is:
	a. Valuation by a recruitment agency or recruitment consultant agreeable to all parties.
	b. Appeal (with resolution) subject to a vote at General Meeting;

Clause	Article Text
	c. [EXTERNAL MEDIATION SERVICE]
	In the event that a labour contract revaluation leads to a breach of the ratio between the highest and lowest paid member of staff (as set in clause 34(c)) the revaluation will only be applied if Labour Shareholders pass a Class Resolution adjusting the ratio to permit the new level of pay. Until such time as a Class Resolution is passed, the maximum pay permissible is capped in accordance with the current ratio (e.g. if the ratio is 3:1, the maximum pay is 3x the lowest paid).
50.	**Relationship Disputes.** In the event of a dispute between two or more members, the escalation procedure is:
	a. Mediation by the President, or a Director, a management consultant, trade union official, Social Enterprise Europe Director; FairShares Association Founder, Regional Social Enterprise Network official or other third-party agreeable to all parties;
	b. Appeal (with resolution) subject to a vote at General Meeting;
	c. [EXTERNAL MEDIATION SERVICE]
51.	Except in the case of resignation or voluntary termination by both parties, a member's employment, supplier contract (or company membership) may be terminated only after an Ordinary Resolution proposing the termination of the contract has been passed in General Meeting.
	a. Termination is subject to the satisfaction of all lawful terms contained in the member's employment and/or trading contract(s). A resolution to terminate an employment or supplier contract, or company membership, cannot be modified by Class Resolution to become a Special Resolution (clause 25 does not apply).
52.	The Company may pay for Directors' and officers' indemnity insurance against liabilities related to Company business, excluding negligence and/or fraud.
53.	**Intellectual Property (IP).** The Company shall record which members have created and contributed intellectual property (IP) to further company objects, and ensure that ownership of all IP remains vested in its creator(s). For the avoidance of doubt, the Company shall not own IP created by members before, during or after their period of membership unless ownership is freely and voluntarily transferred by those members to the Company.
	a. All IP created by members while working for the Company will be vested in them individually and/or collectively.
	b. As a condition of membership and/or employment, all IP created by members during their work for the Company shall be licensed to the Company under a Creative Commons Licence for both non-commercial and commercial trading, with

Clause		Article Text
		permission to adapt, share and re-use the IP in product and service development. Any product or service offered will use the same Creative Commons licence unless a variation of this is negotiated with the creator(s) of the IP.
	i.	Where a member creates (or members create) IP for the Company during their period of membership, the Company shall have an exclusive right to use and commercialise the IP while they remain a member. If the member leaves the Company, upon termination of their membership, the Company shall retain a non-exclusive right to continue using and adapting their IP in both non-commercial and commercial ventures.
	ii.	Members who leave the Company retain a non-exclusive right to use IP they created for the Company in both non-commercial and commercial ventures.
	c.	IP transferred to the Company by members, and IP bought by the Company from third parties, shall be owned collectively by all members and made freely available to them for non-commercial use and private study.
	d.	The Company shall use its best endeavours to manage IP as if it were an 'intellectual commons' for the benefit of Company members.

	DISSOLUTION
Clause	Article Text
54.	Upon dissolution, a qualified accountant or auditor will calculate the value of **"residual assets"** ([shareholder funds] + [accumulated profit and loss account] + [assets – liabilities]). After satisfaction of all creditors, **residual assets** will be distributed to Investor Shareholders in proportion to their shareholding after satisfying the following requirement:

	a.	If the Company has received grant funding from a public authority, charitable body or other asset-locked social enterprise (e.g. a community benefit society or community interest company), a qualified accountant or auditor will verify the amount of Cooperative Capital, and calculate a **"community dividend fraction"** and **"community dividend"**. The **community dividend fraction** will be calculated using the formula shown in 54 (a) (i). The **community dividend** will be calculated using the formula shown in 54 (a) (ii):
		i. [Cooperative Capital] / ([Cooperative Capital] + [Members' Capital])

Clause	Article Text
	ii. ([Members' Capital] + [profit and loss account] + [other assets]) * [community dividend fraction].

Worked Example – Calculating the Community Dividend

Cooperative Capital	£100,000
Members' Capital	£345,000
Profit and Loss Account	£200,000
Assets - Liabilities	£100,000

Community Dividend Fraction = 100,000 / (100,000 + 345,000) = 22%
Residual Assets = 345,000 + 200,000 + 100,000 = £645k
Community Dividend = £645k * 22% = £144,944

    b. If the total value of **residual assets** is greater than [£5,000], not less than **[community dividend]** will be divided equally between the following bodies:

Organisation Name:
FairShares / CIC Company No:
or Charity / Foundation / Association No:
or Cooperative Registration Number:

Organisation Name:
FairShares / CIC Company No:
or Charity / Foundation / Association No:
or Cooperative Registration Number:

Organisation Name:
FairShares / CIC Company No:
or Charity / Foundation / Association No:
or Cooperative Registration Number:

    c. Any remaining assets will be divided equally between Investor Shareholders in proportion to the number of Investor Shares reported in the company's most recent Annual Return, or as set out in the registration document at Companies House (if no Annual Return has been filed). For the avoidance of doubt, changes in shareholdings since registration (if not filed in an Annual Return), or since the most recent Annual Return, will be ignored for the purposes of calculating the share of residual assets paid out when the Company is dissolved.

    d. In finalising the dissolution of the company, and subject to the requirements of Insolvency Law, debts and payments to creditors and shareholders will be satisfied in the following order:

        i. Outstanding debts to **employees, workers and contractors** (e.g. wages/fees)

Clause		Article Text
	ii.	Outstanding debts to other **priority creditors** (e.g. VAT and taxes)
	iii.	Outstanding debts to **suppliers** (e.g. unpaid supplier invoices)
	iv.	Outstanding debts to **other creditors** (e.g. loan balances)
	v.	Payment of the community dividend
	vi.	Division of remaining **residual assets** to Investor Shareholders.
e.		In the event of a failure to agree within 6 months of dissolution which association(s), cooperative(s) and companies should receive the community dividend, or in the event that the organisations in Clause 54(b) have all closed, the [community dividend] will be donated to the FairShares Association to be reinvested in other FairShares associations, cooperatives and companies.

Instituting Change

Model Rules for a FairShares Cooperative

Registered Under
[COOPERATIVES ACT]

Rules of
[COOPERATIVE NAME]

Clause	Article Text
1	**Definitions.** In these Articles:-
	"the Act" means the [COOPERATIVES ACT] and any amendments in force, including those enacted in the [SUBSEQUENT COOPERATIVES ACT REVISIONS].
	"Cash" includes cheques, electronic fund transfers, IOUs, promissory notes and money orders.
	"Member" a holder of a Labour, User, Investor or Founder Share.
	"Beneficiary" a service user, member holding only Investor Shares, or organisation listed in Clause 54 as a beneficiary of the community dividend.
	"Qualifying Contribution" means a commitment to trade with the Cooperative in a way that meets the criteria for membership. Qualifying contributions are set for Labour Shareholders and User Shareholders only.
	"Quorum" a meeting in which a sufficient number of people are present to take decisions.
	"Ordinary Resolution" means a proposal accepted by a majority of votes cast on a one-shareholder, one-vote basis, irrespective of shareholder class, subject to any adjustments provided for in Clause 23 and 24 of these rules.
	"Class Resolution" means a proposal accepted by a majority of votes cast in one shareholder class on a one-shareholder one-vote basis.
	"Special Resolution" means a proposal accepted by a majority of votes cast in each shareholder class separately, on a one-shareholder one-vote basis, plus at least [75%] of all members irrespective of shareholder class on a one-shareholder one-vote basis.
	"Reserves" exclude the current year's profit and loss account.
	"Labour Shares" are shares owned by a member who makes qualifying labour contributions in the Cooperative, entitling her or him to participate in governance and receive a share of surplus. For the purposes of clarity, any person recognised in UK Employment law as a 'worker' will qualify for Labour Shares if they make a qualifying contribution.

Clause	Article Text
	"User Shares" are shares owned by a member who makes a qualifying contribution through their trading or usage of the cooperative's products / services, entitling her or him to participate in governance and receive a share of surplus. For the purposes of clarity, any person recognised as a beneficiary or a customer of the organisation will qualify for User Shares if they make a qualifying contribution.
	"Investor Shares" are shares owned by a member who invests unremunerated labour or equity capital entitling him or her to a share of the Cooperative's assets and surplus.
	"Founder Shares" are shares owned by a Cooperative founder, entitling them to govern the Cooperative.
	"IPS" is a former Industrial and Provident Society, now a Cooperative Society
	"CIC" is a Community Interest Company.
2	Regulations in [COMPANIES ACT] do not apply unless they are referenced directly in these rules, or are required by the Act.
3	The name of the Cooperative is [COOPERATIVE NAME]
4	The registered office of the Cooperative is [ADDRESS] in [REGULATING TERRITORY].
5	The Cooperative's objects are:
	a. to engage in commerce and social activities that spreads wealth and power amongst the Cooperative's primary stakeholders (producers, employees, customers and service users);
	b. to pursue trading activities that are economically, socially and environmentally sustainable, and which improve the well-being of the Cooperative's primary stakeholders;
	c. to promote the development of social entrepreneurship;
	d. to advance Cooperative Values and Principles that create social capital through participatory management and democratic governance processes;
	e. to abide by the internationally recognised values and principles of cooperative identity as defined by the International Cooperative Alliance (ICA), in particular the values of self-help, self-responsibility, democracy, equality and solidarity and the ethical values of honesty, openness, social responsibility and caring for others;
	f to abide by principles of equality of opportunity and oppose forms of discrimination on the grounds of social class, race, ethnic origin, gender, sexual preference, age, disability and religion;
	g. [Add other social / community / public benefit objectives here].

Instituting Change

Clause	Article Text
6	The liability of members is limited.
7	The Cooperative has the power to do anything which is conducive to the furtherance of its objects subject to constraints specified in these rules.
8	The Cooperative's initial share capital is [£1]:
	a. [1] Founder Share(s) of nominal value £1
9	These rules may be altered only by Special Resolution of all shareholder classes, i.e. passed by a majority of votes cast in each shareholder class separately and an overall [75%] of members in favour, on a one-shareholder, one-vote basis.

	MEMBERSHIP, CAPITAL AND FAIRSHARES BRANDING
Clause	Article Text
10	**Membership and Share Capital:** The Cooperative is open to applications for membership in the appropriate class without discrimination, subject to making a qualifying contribution agreed by members in General Meeting. A list of qualifying contributions will be made available to current and prospective members, and will specify: the conditions under which a Labour and/or User share will be issued; the transactions with the Cooperative that qualify an applicant for membership in each class:
	• If there are qualifying contributions for both Labour and User Shares, the Cooperative may be branded as a FairShares Solidarity Cooperative.
	• If there are qualifying contributions for User Shares, but no qualifying contributions for Labour Shares, the Cooperative may be branded as a FairShares User Cooperative.
	• If there are qualifying contributions for Labour Shares, but no qualifying contributions for User Shares, the Cooperative may be branded as a FairShares Worker Cooperative.
	• If there are no qualifying contributions for either User or Labour Shares, the Cooperative is not a FairShares Cooperative / Solidarity Cooperative, and shall not be entitled to use FairShares Branding, or call itself a FairShares Cooperative.
	a. The rights and conditions attaching to shares are:
	i. Founder Shares: issued at a £1 par value to the natural or legal persons who found the cooperative; non-transferable; one vote per shareholder at General Meetings (except as defined in Clauses 23 and 24); 1p fixed preference dividend; forfeited on holder's death, bankruptcy or insolvency; cancelled without payment on winding up.

Clause		Article Text
	ii.	Labour Shares: issued at par value to natural or legal persons who make at least one qualifying contribution in respect of labour provided to the Cooperative; issued in proportion to their labour contribution; non-transferable; one vote per shareholder at General Meetings; forfeited on holder's death, bankruptcy or insolvency; cancelled upon cessation of contracts pertaining to their labour contribution; cancelled without payment on winding up.
	iii.	User Shares: issued at par value to natural or legal persons who make a qualifying contribution in the use of the Cooperative's products and services; non-transferable; one vote per shareholder at General Meetings; forfeited on holder's death, bankruptcy or insolvency; cancelled upon the cessation of a trading relationship; cancelled without payment on winding up.
	iv.	Investor Shares: issued to any natural or legal person (subject to the statutory maximum allowed by the Act at the time of issue); issued at a par value of £1 to investors of equity capital upon payment; issued as 'Member Shares' to providers of labour in proportion to the Capital Gain created by their labour; issued as 'Member Shares' to customers / service users in proportion to the Capital Gain created by their trading activity; one vote per shareholder in General Meeting; withdrawable after [3] years or termination of membership or retirement or death.
	v.	Investor Shares only may be gifted to any of the following:
		1. An FairShares Labour Association, Employee Benefit Trust or other Cooperative Society established for the purpose of managing them for the benefit of the Cooperative's employees;
		2. A FairShares Solidarity Association, Charitable Trust, Charitable Company or Charitable Incorporated Organisation established for the purpose of managing them for public benefit;
		3. A FairShares User Association, Community Interest Company, Community Benefit Society, FairShares Cooperative or FairShares Company created for the purpose of managing them for community benefit.

Instituting Change

Clause	Article Text
	vi. For the avoidance of doubt, upon death, a member's Founder, User and Labour shares are cancelled without payment, and the member's Investor Shares will be redeemed at par value, then paid into their estate for the benefit of their next of kin. **A member's next of kin may not inherit Investor Shares.**
	vii. For the avoidance of doubt, each member has only one vote at General Meetings, irrespective of the number of shares and number of share classes held.
	b. **Alteration of Share Capital.** The Cooperative may issue only new Labour, User or Investor Shares.
11.	**Withdrawal of Investor Shares.**
	a. Providing a member is not in debt to the Cooperative, their Investor Shares may be withdrawn under the following terms using capital in the Cooperative's Redemption Fund. The Redemption Fund is limited to one half of the Cooperative's Reserves at the start of the accounting period.
	i. If the Redemption Fund contains no funds, members' Investor Shares may not be withdrawn except to settle a claim by a member's next of kin following the member's death.
	ii. Investor Shares can be withdrawn after [3] years, on termination of membership or retirement or death or insolvency.
	iii. If the Redemption Fund contains insufficient funds to satisfy all withdrawal requests, the members holding Investor Shares longest will be settled first.
	iv. Investor Shares gifted to institutions in accordance with Clause 10 (a) (iv) cannot be withdrawn.
	b. The 5 members who have traded the most Investor Shares over the last 5 years should be listed, together with their contact details, at the start of the register of members.
	c. Nothing in these articles requires title to securities to be evidenced or transferred by a written instrument if the Act permits otherwise.
12.	**Equity Capital Stakes.**
	The number of Investor Shares (equity) that can be bought or allocated to a member is capped by the Act. Subject to this cap, the following rules apply:
	a. Every natural and legal person (director, employee, supplier or self-employed contractor) who makes a qualifying contribution will be offered Labour Shares proportionate to their qualifying contributions at the end of their probationary period. They will

Clause		Article Text
		also be offered a chance to purchase Investor Shares to the value of [15%] of their initial labour contract (i.e. a person's annual salary, or projected annual value of the contract for services) after 366 days (1 year + 1 day) of continuous service;
	b.	Every natural and legal person (user, customer) who makes a qualifying contribution will be offered User Shares in proportion to their qualifying contributions. They will also be offered a chance to purchase Investor Shares to the value of [15%] of the value of their product and service purchases from the Cooperative;
	c.	The Cooperative may organise a third-party loan or grant of money for an existing member for the purpose of establishing their Investor Shareholding;
	d.	Subject to special resolution, the provisions in clauses 12 (a) and (b) can be applied to other legal entities (companies, cooperatives, associations, charities etc.) who support the work of the Cooperative;
	e.	The Management Committee (MC) shall not be entitled to withhold share offers or prevent share transfers, or reject applications for membership, on the grounds of social class, age, politics, race, creed, religion, culture, ethnic origin, sex or sexual orientation, marital status or disability.
13.		**Valuation.**
	a.	Pre-emption rights are excluded.
	b.	The Cooperative is valued at the start of every financial year, and this is the "Reference Value".
	c.	At incorporation, the Reference Value of the Cooperative is £0.
	d.	Thereafter, the Reference Value shall be calculated as the book value of fixed assets plus 20 (twenty) times the Investor Share for the previous accounting period (see Clause 44).
	e.	A Class Resolution can require revaluation of the Cooperative or any of its assets.
14		**Share Issues.**
	a.	The Cooperative may only issue new Labour, User or Investor shares at par value.
15		Capital Gains **and** Member Shares.
	a.	The "Capital Gain Fraction" is 0.5, and may be changed only by special resolution.
	b.	If the Cooperative's value at the end of an accounting period (the **"New Value"**) is greater than its Reference Value, then **Capital Gain** = (New Value – Reference Value) x [Capital Gain Fraction] and:

Instituting Change

Clause	Article Text
	the "Workers' Gain" is Capital Gain / 2;
	the "Users' Gain" is Capital Gain / 2;
	Member Shares equals 1 share for each £1 of Capital Gain;
	This number of Member Shares shall be issued as Investor Shares to Labour and User Shareholders by any of the following means:
	i. Issuing new Investor Shares to the value of Workers' Gain credited as fully paid to those holding Labour Shares in proportion to the number of Labour Shares held at the commencement of the accounting period;
	ii. Issuing new Investor Shares to the value of Users' Gain credited as fully paid to those holding User Shares in proportion to the number of User Shares held at the commencement of the accounting period;
	iii. Transferring the ownership of Investor Shares (with compensation at par value) from existing Investor Shareholders who wish to sell to Labour Shareholders in proportion to the number of Labour Shares held at the commencement of the accounting period, capped at the Workers' Gain;
	iv. Transferring the ownership of Investor Shares (with compensation at par value) from existing investor shareholders who wish to sell to User Shareholders in proportion to the number of User Shares held at the commencement of the accounting period, capped at the Users' Gain;
	v. Any combination of 15 i) to iv) that has the effect of acquiring for Labour and User Shareholders the number of 'Member Shares' to which they are entitled.

Worked Example – Calculating the Capital Gain and Member Shares

Investor Shares Issued:	45,000
Capital Gain Fraction:	0.5 (50%)
Reference Value:	£60,000
New Value:	£75,000
Capital Gain	£7,500 (75,000 – 60,000 = 15,000, then multiply by 50% to get 7,500)
Workers' Gain:	= £7,500/ 2 = £3,750
Users' Gain:	= £7,500 / 2 = £3,750
Number of Member Shares:	= 7,500
Investor Shares (Revised):	45,000 + 7,500 = 52,500

The maximum shareholding of each member is capped by the Act – at the time of writing this was [number].

Clause	Articles
16	**Borrowing and Investment.**
	a. **Borrowing:** the Management Committee (MC) may exercise all the powers of the Cooperative to borrow money at commercial rates, and to mortgage or charge its undertaking, property and assets (present or future) and to issue debentures provided that:
	i. No borrowing is authorised that exceeds the value of the Reserves unless:
	1. The lender does not take a charge over the assets of the Cooperative;
	2. the loan amount or credit agreement is unsecured (i.e. does not require the Cooperative to offer security);
	3. the borrowing secures for the Cooperative an asset or contract with a value greater than the amount borrowed.
	ii. The borrowing is authorised by an Ordinary Resolution.
	b. **Commercial Investments:** the MC may exercise all the powers of the Cooperative to make commercial investments, provided that the sum invested does not exceed one half of Reserves.
	i. The balance of Reserves must be held in current or deposit accounts, low-risk stocks, bonds or accessible savings accounts.
	c. **Social investments** may be made each year in accordance with Clause 10(v) providing they total no more than one half of the opening balance of the Redemption Fund for that year.

GOVERNANCE	
Clause	Articles
17	The Management Committee (MC) may call General Meetings and, on the requisition of members holding a tenth or more of the shares in any class, must convene a General Meeting for a date not later than 4 weeks after receipt of the requisition. General Meetings can take place through an online collaborative decision-making platform using technology agreed by members.
18	In each financial year, a minimum of one General Meeting will be held in addition to the Annual General Meeting (AGM).
	a. No business shall be transacted at a General Meeting unless a quorum of members is present. Unless and until otherwise decided by General Meeting, two-fifths of the membership shall be the quorum, subject to the number of members being more than [10] and less than [50].

Instituting Change

Clause	Articles	
	b.	In the event of the membership exceeding [50] the quorum shall be [20].
	c.	In the event of the membership being less than [10], the quorum shall be one-half subject to a minimum of [3].
	d.	An invitation to all members to join an online collaborative decision-making platform before a General Meeting shall be sufficient to satisfy the rules regarding a quorum providing all resolutions on which a vote is required are posted to the online collaborative decision-making platform before the meeting.
	e.	No business shall be transacted at an off-line General Meeting until the meeting has agreed a chairperson. Online General Meetings will not require a chairperson. Whenever a President is in post, the President will chair an off-line General Meeting. If a President is not in post, or the President is not present, the meeting will elect one of the MC members to chair the meeting. If no MC member is present, the meeting may elect a chairperson from those present.
19.	The General Meeting can set corporate policy, approve/reject social enterprise plans, and take decisions about acquisition and disposal of property, and partnership arrangements with other organisations.	
	a.	A proposal to acquire another organisation may be taken by Ordinary Resolution.
	b.	A proposal to merge or sell the Cooperative must be put as a Special Resolution.
	c.	A proposal to wind up or dissolve the Cooperative must be put as a Special Resolution.
20	Corporate policy and social enterprise plans are implemented by a Chief Executive Officer or Executive Team appointed by MC Members. The MC will stipulate their authority whenever appointed.	
	a.	When no Chief Executive Officer or Executive Team is in post, the MC member with the most Labour Shares will assume the responsibilities of the Chief Executive Officer until a new Chief Executive Officer or Executive Team can be appointed.
	b.	If the situation in 20(a) arises, and two or more MC members have the same number of Labour Shares, the longest serving member will assume the responsibilities of the Chief Executive Officer until a new Chief Executive Officer or Executive Team is appointed.
	c.	The Chief Executive Officer or Executive Team is responsible to the General Meeting and MC for the organisation and management of the cooperative and the implementation of the Cooperative's social enterprise plans.

Clause	Articles
21.	Every Founder, Labour, User and Investor shareholder can attend, speak and propose resolutions at a General Meeting, can stand (subject to clauses 30 and 31) for election as an MC member and can cast one vote at General Meetings (except as provided for in clauses 23 and 24).
22.	Any person can act as a proxy for a member at General Meeting. An instrument appointing a proxy must be written in a usual form, or a form approved by the MC.
	a. A proxy may act for a maximum of one other member at General Meetings (i.e. can cast a maximum of two votes, including their own).
23.	Decisions at off-line General Meetings are made by passing resolutions with a show of hands, unless a poll is demanded by at least 2 members. At online General Meetings, decisions are made by approving a member proposal using the collaborative decision-making tools adopted by members.
	a. For Ordinary Resolutions taken by a show of hands (or online vote), Founder, Labour, User and Investor shareholders have one vote each, irrespective of the number of shares held and irrespective of the class(es) of share held.
	b. For Ordinary Resolutions where a poll is called, only Labour Shareholders, User Shareholders and Investor Shareholders vote. Each shareholder votes once, irrespective of the number of shares held. Their vote counts toward each shareholder class in which they hold shares. Founder shareholders vote only if they also hold Labour, User and/or Investor Shares.
	c. If a poll is requested by at least 2 members, the chairperson must offer each shareholder class a chance to pass a Class Resolution in accordance with the provisions of Clause 25 before proceeding with the poll.
24.	On a show of hands, online vote, or poll, every member who is present in person or by proxy, has one vote.
	a. In the event of a poll, the total number of labour, user and investor votes for and against the resolution will be recalculated using the following formulae (see clause 44 for [Investor Share Fraction]; see clause 40 for [Labour Share Fraction] and [User Share Fraction]:
	i. [Investor Votes For] / [Investor Votes Cast] * [Investor Share Fraction]
	ii. [Investor Votes Against] / [Investor Votes Cast] * [Investor Share Fraction]
	iii. [Labour Votes For] / [Labour Votes Cast] * [Labour Share Fraction]

Instituting Change

Clause	Articles
	iv. [Labour Votes Against] / [Labour Votes Cast] * [Labour Share Fraction]
	v. [User Votes For] / [User Votes Cast] * [User Share Fraction]
	vi. [User Votes Against] / [User Votes Cast] * [User Share Fraction]
	b. The total vote for the resolution is the aggregate of i), iii) and v)
	c. The total vote against the resolution is the aggregate of ii), iv) and vi)
	d. For the resolution to pass, the aggregate of i), iii) and v) must be greater than 0.5, otherwise the resolution is not passed.
	Worked Example – Taking a Poll for an Ordinary Resolution **at a General Meeting**
	Investor Votes Cast: 30
	Investor Votes For: 18 = 18 / 30 * 30% = 18.0%
	Investor Votes Against: 12 = 12 / 30 * 30% = 12.0%
	Investor Share Fraction 30%
	Labour Votes Cast: 17
	Labour Votes For: 5 = 5 / 17 * 35% = 10.3%
	Labour Votes Against: 12 = 12 / 17 * 35% = 24.7%
	Labour Share Fraction: 35%
	User Votes Cast: 170
	User Votes For: 40 = 40 / 170 * 35% = 8.2%
	User Votes Against: 130 = 130 / 170 * 35% = 26.8%
	User Share Fraction: 35%
	Total For = 18% + 10.3% + 8.2% = 36.5%
	Total Against = 12% + 24.7% + 26.8% = 63.5%
	The resolution is defeated.
25.	A Class Resolution **passed by any shareholder class can amend an Ordinary Resolution so that it becomes a Special Resolution (with the exception of contract terminations described in clause 51).**
	a. A Special Resolution is passed if:
	i. a majority of votes cast in each shareholder class separately (on a one-shareholder one-vote basis) are in favour of the resolution;
	ii. at least [75%] of all members cast their vote in favour of the resolution, irrespective of shareholder class, on a one-shareholder one-vote basis.
26.	Unless a poll is demanded, a declaration by the chairperson at the meeting (or announcement in an online forum by the Cooperative) that a resolution has been carried or lost, and an entry to that effect in the book containing the minutes of the proceedings (or equivalent

Clause	Articles
	record in an online collaborative decision-making forum) shall be conclusive evidence of the fact without proof of the number or proportions of the votes recorded in favour or against a resolution.
27.	A written resolution signed by all members is valid as if properly passed at a General Meeting.
28.	The proceedings of a meeting are not invalidated by the accidental omission to give notice of the meeting to, or the non-receipt of notice of the meeting by, a person entitled to receive notice.
29.	**Management Committee Members (Directors)**. The Cooperative shall have a Management Committee (MC) of between [three] and [nine] directors except in the following circumstances:
	a. The cooperative is in receipt of grant or loan funding from a public authority, charitable body or other asset-locked organisation (e.g. a credit union, community cooperative or community interest cooperative), in which case the minimum number of directors shall be three representing at least two shareholder classes, with at least one financial specialist.
	b. The cooperative has [50] or more members, in which case the minimum number of MC members shall be five with at least one representing each shareholder class, with at least one financial specialist.
30.	If the Cooperative has fewer than [50] members, MC members will be proposed by the Founders or existing MC members and approved by Ordinary Resolution.
	a. MC members may freely negotiate contracts of any value until the Cooperative files its first set of accounts. Thereafter, MC members may freely negotiate contracts to the value of [25%] of the cooperative's annual turnover (as reported in the previous year's filed accounts). Contracts in excess of this amount require General Meeting approval.
	b. An MC member may be removed at General Meeting by an Ordinary Resolution.
31.	If the Cooperative has [50] or more members, an MC and a president will be elected annually as follows.
	a. Labour Shareholders will elect a maximum of [two] MC members (one will be subject to re-election by rotation every two-years).
	b. User Shareholders will elect a maximum of [two] MC members (one will be subject to re-election by rotation every two-years).
	c. Investor Shareholders (if applicable) will elect a maximum of [two] MC director (one will be subject to re-election by rotation every two-years).

Instituting Change

Clause	Articles
	d. Founder Shareholders will elect a maximum of [two] MC members, who may be removed only by the provisions set out in 31(f).
	e. A maximum of [one] MC member may be appointed (co-opted) by the other MC members for their specialist financial skills.
	f. An MC member may be removed from office at any General Meeting by a Class Resolution of a shareholder class that elected him or her, or by Ordinary Resolution.
	g. A Cooperative President will be elected from the MC members on a poll of all shareholders (one vote per shareholder) at the Annual General Meeting. The President has a non-executive role in the running of the Cooperative, and is responsible for overseeing board meetings, maintaining the public image of the Cooperative, and facilitating good communications between MC members and cooperative members. The President has a casting vote at board and General Meetings, but is not required to use it.
	h. In the absence of a President, or if a President is not elected, the holder(s) of Founder Shares will fulfil this role (as set out in 31(g)).
	i. An MC member cannot be removed by other MC members except at General Meeting (as set out in 31 (f)).
	j. Cooperative directors may freely negotiate contracts to the value of [12.5%] of the Cooperative's annual turnover (as reported in the previous year's filed accounts). Contracts in excess of this amount require General Meeting approval.
32.	MC meetings may be held between General Meetings by any means defined within the Act, and through an online collaborative decision-making platform.
	a. All acts done by any meeting of the MC or by any person acting as a member of the MC, even if it be afterwards discovered that there was some defect in the appointment of any MC member or person acting as such, or that they or any of them were disqualified, be as valid as if every such person had been duly appointed and was qualified to be an MC member.

EXPENSES, BENEFITS AND PAY	
Clause	Article Text
33.	Providers of labour (MC members, employees, self-employed contractors) shall be paid reasonable expenses wholly incurred in relation to furthering the interests of the Cooperative.
	a. A schedule of acceptable fringe benefits and expenses may be agreed by Ordinary Resolution. Any expenses paid, or fringe

Clause		Article Text
		benefits provided, outside the scope of an agreed schedule must be itemised in the annual accounts.
	b.	Fringe benefits and expenses must be itemised and recorded in such a way that they can be inspected by any member during normal office hours.
34.		**Remuneration** has three components: Basic Wages ("Pay"), Labour Share dividends and Investor Share interest.
	a.	Each provider of labour is subject to one or more contracts (employment contract, contract for services or cooperative membership) which controls the manner in which they are remunerated for their labour. These articles, including subsequent modifications, are part of any contract between the Cooperative and those providing labour (MC members, shareholders, employees, self-employed contractors). All members of the Cooperative shall be provided with a copy of these rules upon agreement or variation of a contract to supply labour.
	b.	Labour may be recognised solely through cooperative membership and remunerated solely through Labour Share dividends. A formal contract of employment will be issued if, in the view of the MC, 'employee status' tests used in employment tribunals have been, or are expected to be, satisfied (i.e. a person works regular hours, receives regular pay, has agreed holiday entitlements and is subject to regular supervision etc.).
	c.	If the Cooperative issues contracts of employment to members of staff, **the maximum ratio between the hourly rate of the highest and lowest paid member of staff shall be [3:1]**. This ratio can only be amended by a Class Resolution in a meeting of Labour Shareholders. This ratio may **not** be amended by Ordinary Resolution.
	d.	At the start of each accounting period, if the Cooperative has any employees, an amount equal to (Basic Wages x Current Inflation Rate) will be set aside for increases in Basic Wages. The application of any remuneration system to employees and self-employed contractors is at the discretion of the CEO or Executive Team (unless overridden by the procedure set out in clause 49). If the budget for increases in remuneration is not distributed within an accounting period, any unused part **must** be distributed as Investor Shares in proportion to Labour Shareholdings.
	e.	An increase in the budget set in 34(d) can only be passed by Special Resolution.

Instituting Change

Clause		Article Text
	f.	MC members' pay and conditions follow the same principles as other cooperative members and employees.
35.	a.	**"Total Revenue"** means sales plus earnings from services provided plus any other income, but excludes proceeds of new issues of securities or loans obtained
	b.	**"Profit"** is equal to Total Revenue less the cost of materials and services, less depreciation, less rents, less interest.
36.		**"Associated Costs"** means the costs directly associated with a given amount of Pay, including employee's and employer's contributions to insurance schemes, superannuation, healthcare plan, childcare, staff club and any other benefits deducted from pay, together with sickness, maternity, paternity or other statutory pay, and Pay-As-You-Earn income tax.
37.		**"Surplus"** is equal to Profit, less Pay including their Associated Costs, less Corporation Tax.
	a.	The first [£10,000] of Surplus or 30% of Profits (whichever is greater) will be allocated to Reserves as working capital. This amount will be deducted from Surplus before calculating User Share Dividends, Labour Share Dividends and Investor Share interest
	b.	Half of the Surplus transferred to Reserves will be held in a **"Redemption Fund"** to satisfy member requests to withdraw Investor Shares as set out in Clause 11.
38.		Additional Capital Expenditure, Extraordinary and Research and Development Costs in excess of [£5,000] not financed by a fundraising campaign must either:
	a.	be deducted from Surplus, or
	b.	be paid for from Reserves,
		or as determined by Special Resolution or a qualified accountant. Any member may ask a qualified accountant to determine if an item comes under these categories.
39.		**"Labour Share"** and **"User Share"**. The Labour and User Share of Surplus, distributed in dividends, is calculated by multiplying [Surplus] (if greater than zero) for the relevant period by the [Labour Share Fraction] and [User Share Fraction]. If [Surplus] is less than or equal to zero, no Labour Share or User Share dividends are paid.
	a.	In the event that there are no Labour Shareholders to pay dividends, the Cooperative shall establish or increase a restricted fund to the value of the Labour Share. The MC may exercise discretion on how to allocate the restricted fund to projects that improve the well-being of the Cooperative's workforce.

Clause	Article Text
	b. In the event that there are no User Shareholders to pay dividends, the Cooperative shall establish or increase a restricted fund to the value of the User Share. The MC may exercise discretion on how to allocate the restricted fund to projects that improve the well-being of the Cooperative's users.
40.	"Labour Share Fraction" and "User Share Fraction"
	a. The Labour Share Fraction is [0.35] and User Share Fraction is [0.35] and may be changed only by Special Resolution. If the Labour Share Fraction or User Share Fraction is decreased, Investor Shares credited as fully paid at the fair price must be given to holders of Labour and User Shares in proportion to the projected loss of dividends for the next 3 years.
	b. No Labour or User Shareholder may receive a dividend of more than [Surplus] x [Labour Share Fraction].
41.	**"Labour Share Dividends"** and **"User Share Dividends"**
	At the end of an accounting period, the Labour Share and User Share are distributed as dividends to each Labour and User shareholder using the following formulae:
	[Labour Share] x (Member's Labour Shareholding / All Issued Labour Shares).
	[User Share] x (Member's User Shareholding / All Issued User Shares).
42.	At the discretion of the MC, members and employees may be advanced a proportion of their projected Labour Share dividends on a regular basis in addition to monthly Pay. Advances must be listed in the Annual Accounts and deducted from the Labour Share before calculating Labour Share Dividends.
43.	Providers of labour (MC members, employees, self-employed contractors) may, subject to mutual consent, be part-paid by the issue of Investor Shares, credited as fully paid.
44.	Investor Share Interest is paid after Labour and User Share dividends.
	a. The "Investor Share Fraction" is [0.30] and the "Investor Share" is [Surplus] x [Investor Share Fraction]. This may be changed only by special resolution.
	b. No dividends are paid on Investor Shares. Interest is payable subject to a cap which is calculated as follows: [Surplus] x [Investor Share Fraction] x (1 – [Capital Gain Fraction].

Instituting Change

Clause	Article Text
	c. Interest is divided *pro rata* between all Investor Shareholders based on the number of Investor Shares held by each member *before* Member Shares are allocated for the same accounting period.
	d. The interest must be paid within 6 calendar months of the end of the accounting period. Interest at the Cooperative's Bank overdraft rate is to accumulate on unpaid amounts after this time.
45.	**Cash Instead of Investor Shares.** The MC can offer all Investor Shareholders a chance to receive cash payments instead of taking their Member Shares as new Investor Shares.
46.	No additional sum may be transferred from the profit and loss account to Reserves unless it represents new Investor Shares credited as fully-paid, or is approved by special resolution, or is required by law.
	ACCOUNTING AND AUDITING

47.	Financial and social accounts will be prepared for MC and General Meetings by a person with appropriate bookkeeping and accounting skills / qualifications. They will use accounting conventions agreed by the MC, or as required by the Act. Any member or person authorised in writing by a member may inspect the accounting records during normal working hours.
	a. If the Cooperative has fewer than [50] members, the Board may put an ordinary resolution to the General meeting to approve one of the following:
	   i. **Either:** the appointment of independent accountants and/or auditors to undertake financial and social audits;
	   ii. **Or:** an application for exemption from audit under the relevant accounting regulations;
	b. If the Cooperative has [50] or more members:
	   i. The board shall recommend a choice of financial and social auditors for approval in General Meeting.
	   ii. The selected financial auditor shall audit the cooperative's financial accounts prior to their approval in General Meeting for filing with the relevant regulatory authority.
	   iii. The selected social auditor shall assist with audit of the internal democracy and decision-making of the Cooperative, the wages, health and safety, skill sharing and educational opportunities of its members and employees, or other matters concerning overall personal or job satisfaction; an assessment of the Cooperative's activities externally, including effects on people, the environment and other organisations.

Clause	Article Text
	iv. An audit committee of up to four people (comprising non-MC members from at least two shareholder classes) will be elected at each AGM.
	v. The purpose of the audit committee is:
	1. to assist and check the preparation of financial records presented to General Meetings so that they are accurate, authentic and meet the needs of members;
	2. to assist and check the preparation of the information needed for a social audit;
	3. to organise elections in accordance with Clause 31;
	4. to record, check and authenticate that the procedures in clauses 17 to 27 are being followed when voting takes place in a General Meeting.
48.	Accountants, Auditors and Independent Experts. These must be chosen by ordinary resolution.
	a. The financial auditor (if appointed) shall be from a Recognised Qualifying Body (RQB).
	b. Accountants, Auditors and Independent Experts shall require the accounts to record Members Capital and Community Capital separately.
	i. **"Members' Capital"** is defined as the sum of the value of members' Investor Shareholdings.
	ii. **"Cooperative Capital"** is defined as the sum of grants and donations received from public authorities, charitable bodies and other asset-locked social enterprises (e.g. community benefit societies or community interest companies), plus any capital that members' are required by the Act to convert, or have voluntarily converted, to Cooperative Capital.

DISPUTE RESOLUTION AND INTELLECTUAL PROPERTY	
Clause	Article Text
49.	**Labour Contract Revaluations.** In the event of a dispute, the escalation procedure is:
	a. Valuation by a recruitment agency or recruitment consultant agreeable to all parties.
	b. Appeal (with resolution) subject to a vote at General Meeting;
	c. [EXTERNAL MEDIATION SERIVCE]
	In the event that a labour contract revaluation leads to a breach of the ratio between the highest and lowest paid member of staff (as set in clause 34(c)) the revaluation will only be applied if Labour

Instituting Change

Clause	Article Text
	Shareholders pass a Class Resolution adjusting the ratio to permit the new level of pay. Until such time as a Class Resolution is passed, the maximum pay permissible is capped in accordance with the current ratio (e.g. if the ratio is 3:1, the maximum pay is 3x the lowest paid).
50.	**Relationship Disputes.** In the event of a dispute between two or more members, the escalation procedure is:
	a. Mediation by the President, or MC member, a management consultant, trade union official, Co-operative Body official, Social Enterprise Europe Director, FairShares Association Founder, or other third-party agreeable to all parties;
	b. Appeal (with resolution) subject to a vote at General Meeting;
	c. [EXTENAL MEDIATION SERVICE]
51.	Except in the case of resignation or voluntary termination by both parties, a member's employment, supplier contract (or cooperative membership) may be terminated only after an Ordinary Resolution proposing the termination of the contract has been passed in General Meeting.
	a. Termination is subject to the satisfaction of all lawful terms contained in the member's employment and/or trading contract(s). A resolution to terminate an employment or supplier contract, or cooperative membership, cannot be modified by Class Resolution to become a Special Resolution (clause 25 does not apply).
52.	The Cooperative may pay for MC members' and officers' indemnity insurance against liabilities related to Cooperative business, excluding negligence and/or fraud.
53.	**Intellectual Property (IP).** The Cooperative shall record which members have created and contributed intellectual property (IP) to further cooperative objects, and ensure that ownership of all IP remains vested in its creator(s). For the avoidance of doubt, the Cooperative shall not own IP created by members before, during or after their period of membership unless ownership is freely and voluntarily transferred by those members to the Cooperative.
	a. All IP created by members while working for the Cooperative will be vested in them individually and/or collectively.
	b. As a condition of membership and/or employment, all IP created by members during their work for the Cooperative shall be licensed to the Cooperative under a Creative Commons Licence for both non-commercial and commercial trading, with permission to adapt, share and re-use the IP in product and service development. Any product or service offered will use the same Creative Commons licence unless a variation of this is negotiated with the creator(s) of the IP.

Clause	Article Text	
	i.	Where a member creates (or members create) IP for the Cooperative during their period of membership, the Cooperative shall have an exclusive right to use and commercialise the IP while they remain a member. If the member leaves the Cooperative, upon termination of their membership, the Cooperative shall retain a non-exclusive right to continue using and adapting their IP in both non-commercial and commercial ventures.
	ii.	Members who leave the Cooperative retain a non-exclusive right to use IP they created for the Cooperative in both non-commercial and commercial ventures.
	c.	IP transferred to the Cooperative by members, and IP bought by the Cooperative from third parties, shall be owned collectively by all members and made freely available to them for non-commercial use and private study.
	d.	The Cooperative shall use its best endeavours to manage IP as if it were an 'intellectual commons' for the benefit of Cooperative members.
	DISSOLUTION	
54.	Upon dissolution, a qualified accountant or auditor will calculate the value of **"residual assets"** ([members' capital] + [accumulated profit and loss account] + [assets – liabilities]). After satisfaction of all creditors, **residual assets** will be distributed to Investor Shareholders in proportion to their shareholding after satisfying the following requirement:	
	a.	If the Cooperative has received grant funding from a public authority, charitable body or other asset-locked social enterprise (e.g. a community benefit society or community interest cooperative), a qualified accountant or auditor will verify the amount of Cooperative Capital, and calculate a **"community dividend fraction"** and **"community dividend"**. The **community dividend fraction** will be calculated using the formula shown in 54 (a) (i). The **community dividend** will be calculated using the formula shown in 54 (a) (ii):
	i.	[Cooperative Capital] / ([Cooperative Capital] + [Members' Capital])
	ii.	([Members' Capital] + [profit and loss account] + [other assets]) * [community dividend fraction].

Instituting Change

Worked Example – Calculating the Community Dividend

Cooperative Capital	£100,000
Members' Capital	£345,000
Profit and Loss Account	£200,000
Assets - Liabilities	£100,000

Community Dividend Fraction = 100,000 / (100,000 + 345,000) = 22%
Residual Assets = 345,000 + 200,000 + 100,000 = £645k
Community Dividend = £645k * 22% = £144,944

    b.   If the total value of **residual assets** is greater than [£5,000], not less than **[community dividend]** will be divided equally between the following bodies:

Organisation Name:
FairShares / CIC No:
or Charity / Foundation / Association No:
or Cooperative Registration Number:

Organisation Name:
FairShares / CIC No:
or Charity / Foundation / Association No:
or Cooperative Registration Number:

Organisation Name:
FairShares / CIC No:
or Charity / Foundation / Association No:
or Cooperative Registration Number:

    c.   Any remaining assets will be divided equally between Investor Shareholders **in proportion to number of shares held at the end of the previous year's trading.** For the avoidance of doubt, changes in balances since the previous year end will be ignored for the purposes of calculating the share of residual assets paid out when the Cooperative is dissolved.

    d.   In finalising the dissolution of the Cooperative, and subject to the requirements of Insolvency Law, debts and payments to creditors and shareholders will be satisfied in the following order:

        i.   Outstanding debts to **employees, workers and contractors** (e.g. wages/fees)

        ii.   Outstanding debts to other **priority creditors** (e.g. VAT and taxes)

        iii.   Outstanding debts to **suppliers** (e.g. unpaid supplier invoices)

        iv.   Outstanding debts to **other creditors** (e.g. loan balances)

        v.   Payment of the community dividend

vi. Division of remaining **residual assets** to Investor Shareholders.

e. In the event of a failure to agree within 6 months of dissolution which association(s), cooperative(s) and companies should receive the community dividend, or in the event that the organisations in Clause 54(b) have all closed, the [community dividend] will be donated to FairShares Association Ltd to be reinvested in other FairShares associations, cooperatives and companies.

Instituting Change

Model Rules for a FairShares Association

Registered Under
[COMPANIES / ASSOCIATIONS / SOCIETIES ACT]

Rules of
[ASSOCIATION NAME]

Clause	Article Text
1	**Definitions.** In these Articles:-
	"the Act" means the [ASSOCIATIONS ACT] and any amendments in force, including those enacted in the [SUBSEQUENT ASSOCIATIONS ACT REVISIONS].
	"Cash" includes cheques, electronic fund transfers, IOUs, promissory notes and money orders.
	"Member" a Labour, User or Founder Member.
	"Beneficiary" includes organisations listed in Clause 54 as a beneficiary of the community dividend.
	"Qualifying Contribution" means a commitment to trade with the Association in a way that meets the criteria for membership. Qualifying contributions are set for Labour Members and User Members only.
	"Quorum" a meeting in which a sufficient number of people are present to take decisions.
	"Ordinary Resolution" means a proposal accepted by a majority of votes cast on a one-member, one-vote basis, irrespective of member class, subject to any adjustments provided for in Clause 23 and 24 of these rules.
	"Class Resolution" means a proposal accepted by a majority of votes cast in one member class on a one-member, one-vote basis.
	"Special Resolution" means a proposal accepted by a majority of votes cast in each member class separately, on a one-member, one-vote basis, plus at least [75%] of all members on a one-member one-vote basis.
	"Reserves" exclude the current year's profit and loss account.
	"Labour Member" is a member who makes qualifying labour contributions in the Association, entitling her or him to participate in Association governance and to allocate a share of surpluses to projects developed by the association. For the purposes of clarity, any person recognised in UK Employment law as a 'worker' will be eligible for Labour Membership if they make a qualifying contribution.

Clause	Article Text
	"User Member" is a member who has made a qualifying contribution as a user of the Association's products / services, entitling her or him to participate in Association governance and allocate a share of the surpluses to projects developed by the association. For the purposes of clarity, any person recognised as a beneficiary or a customer of the organisation will be eligible for User Membership if they make a qualifying contribution.
	"Funder" is an individual or organisation that invests or donates financial capital to support the Association's objectives.
	"Founder Member" is a person who established the Association and who, by virtue of being a founder, has specific rights to contribute to its governance.
	"IPS" is a former Industrial and Provident Society, now a Cooperative Society
	"CIC" is a Community Interest Company.
2	The Association is subject to statutory regulation according to the Act used for its incorporation.
3	The name of the Association is [ASSOCIATION NAME]
4	The registered office of the Association is [ADDRESS] in [REGULATING TERRITORY].
5	The Association's objects are:
	a. to engage in activities that improve the well-being of the Association's primary stakeholders (producers, employees, customers and service users);
	b. to pursue trading activities that are economically, socially and environmentally sustainable, and which improve the well-being of the Association's primary stakeholders;
	c. to promote the development of social entrepreneurship;
	d. to advance Co-operative Values and Principles that create social capital through participatory management and democratic governance processes;
	e. to abide by the internationally recognised values and principles of cooperative identity as defined by the International Cooperative Alliance (ICA), in particular the values of self-help, self-responsibility, democracy, equality and solidarity and the ethical values of honesty, openness, social responsibility and caring for others;
	f to abide by principles of equality of opportunity and oppose forms of discrimination on the grounds of social class, race, ethnic origin, gender, sexual preference, age, disability and religion;
	g. [Add other social / community / public benefit objectives here].

Instituting Change

Clause	Article Text
6	The liability of members is limited, as defined by the Act used to incorporate the Association.
7	The Association has the power to do anything which is conducive to the furtherance of its objects subject to constraints specified in these rules.
8	The Association has no share capital.
9	These rules may be altered only by Special Resolution of all member classes, i.e. passed by a majority of votes cast in each member class separately and an overall [75%] of members in favour, on a one-shareholder, one-vote basis.

MEMBERSHIP, CAPITAL AND FAIRSHARES BRANDING

Clause	Article Text
10	**Membership and Share Capital:** The Association is open to applications for membership in the appropriate class without discrimination, subject to making a qualifying contribution agreed by members in General Meeting. A list of qualifying contributions will be made available to current and prospective members, and will specify: the conditions under which a Labour and/or User share will be issued; the transactions with the Association that qualify an applicant for membership in each class: • If there are qualifying contributions for both Labour and User Members, the Association may brand itself as a FairShares Solidarity Association. • If there are qualifying contributions for User Members, but no qualifying contributions for Labour Members, the Association may brand itself as a FairShares User Association. • If there are qualifying contributions for Labour Members, but no qualifying contributions for User Members, the Association may brand itself as a FairShares Labour Association. • If there are no qualifying contributions for either User or Labour Members, the Association shall not be entitled to use FairShares Branding, or call itself a FairShares Association. a. Members who satisfy membership criteria shall be accepted as Labour and/or User Members reflecting their contribution to the Association within the terms set out on the Association's application form. The rights and conditions attaching to membership are: i. Founder Membership: non-transferable; one vote per member at General Meetings; cancelled on the member's death, bankruptcy or insolvency; cancelled on winding up.

Clause	Article Text		
		ii.	**Labour Membership:** offered to natural or legal persons who make at least one qualifying contribution in respect of labour provided to the Association; non-transferable; one vote per member at General Meetings; cancelled on holder's death, bankruptcy or insolvency; cancelled upon cessation of the qualifying contribution; cancelled on winding up.
		iii.	**User Membership:** offered to natural or legal persons who make a qualifying contribution through use of the association's products and services; non-transferable; one vote per member at General Meetings; cancelled on member's death, bankruptcy or insolvency; cancelled upon a cessation of the qualifying contribution; cancelled on winding up.
		vi.	For the avoidance of doubt, upon death, a member's Founder, User and Labour memberships are cancelled, and all benefits linked to membership cease.
		vii.	For the avoidance of doubt, each member has only one vote at General Meetings, irrespective of the number of memberships they hold.
	b.	**Alteration of Member Classes.** The Association may not create additional classes of member, and may only offer Labour or User memberships after incorporation.	
11.	**Transfer of Member Benefits.**		
	a.	Subject to the agreement of the Association's Board of Trustees, a member may transfer the benefits (but not the rights) of membership to:	
		i.	An Trust or Co-operative Society established for the benefit of members;
		ii.	A Charitable Trust, Charitable Company or Charitable Incorporated Organisation that creates public benefits consistent with one or more objects of the Association;
		iii.	A Community Interest Company, Community Benefit Society, FairShares Association, FairShares Co-operative or FairShares Company that creates community benefits consistent with one or more objects of the Association.
12.	Equity Capital Stakes.		
	The Association will not issue Equity Capital Stakes (shares) to members or third parties.		
13.	**Valuation.**		
	a.	The Association is valued at the start of every financial year, and this is the "Reference Value".	
	b.	At incorporation, the Reference Value of the Association is £0.	

Instituting Change

Clause		Article Text
	c.	Thereafter, the Reference Value shall be calculated as the book value of fixed assets plus 7 (seven) times the Surplus for the previous accounting period (see Clause 37).
	e.	A Class Resolution can require revaluation of the Association or any of its assets.
14		**Share Purchases**
	a.	The Association may purchase shares in other organisations that support one or more of its objects.
15		Capital Gains **and Member Investor Accounts**
	a.	The **"Capital Gain Fraction"** is 0.5, and may be changed only by special resolution.
	b.	If the Association's value at the end of an accounting period (the **"New Value"**) is greater than its Reference Value, then **Capital Gain** = (New Value – Reference Value) x [Capital Gain Fraction] and:

the "Workers' Gain"   is   Capital Gain / 2;
the "Users' Gain"   is   Capital Gain / 2;
Investor Accounts   £1 credit for each £1 of Capital Gain;

Members' Investor Accounts are restricted funds held for Labour and User Members to allocate to projects developed by the Association's members. Credits to be issues as follows:

i. Credit each Labour Members' Investor Account with [Workers' Gain] / [Number of Labour Members];

ii. Credit [Users' Gain] to a restricted fund controlled collectively by User Members.

Worked Example – Calculating the Capital Gain and Member Shares

Investor Shares Issued: 45,000
Capital Gain Fraction: 0.5 (50%)
Reference Value: £60,000
New Value: £75,000
Capital Gain   £7,500 (75,000 – 60,000 = 15,000, then multiply by 50% to get 7,500)
Workers' Gain: = £7,500/ 2 = £3,750 (allocated individually)
Users' Gain: = £7,500 / 2 = £3,750 (help collectively)
Credits to Investor Accounts: = £7,500

Clause		Article Text
16		**Borrowing and Investment.**
	a.	**Borrowing:** the Board of Trustees may exercise all the powers of the Association to borrow money at commercial rates, and to mortgage or charge its undertaking, property and assets (present or future) and to issue debentures provided that:

Clause		Article Text
	i.	No borrowing is authorised that exceeds the value of the Reserves unless:
		1. The lender does not take a charge over the assets of the Association;
		2. the loan amount or credit agreement is unsecured (i.e. does not require the Association to offer security);
		3. the borrowing secures for the Association an asset or contract with a value greater than the amount borrowed.
	ii.	The borrowing is authorised by an Ordinary Resolution.
	b.	**Commercial Investments:** the Board may exercise all the powers of the Association to make commercial investments, provided that the sum invested does not exceed one half of Reserves.
	i.	The balance of Reserves must be held in current or deposit accounts, low-risk stocks, bonds or accessible savings accounts.
	c.	**Social investments** may be made each year in accordance with the objects of the association providing they total no more than one half of the opening balance of the Redemption Fund for that year.
		GOVERNANCE
17		The Trustee Board may call General Meetings and, on the requisition of 1/10th of members must convene a General Meeting for a date not later than 4 weeks after receipt of the requisition. General Meetings can take place through an online collaborative decision-making platform using technology agreed by members.
18		In each financial year, a minimum of one General Meeting will be held in addition to the Annual General Meeting (AGM). The ability of members to join a General Assembly and vote using online collaborative decision-making tools shall be deemed to satisfy this requirement.
	a.	No business shall be transacted at a General Meeting unless a quorum of members is present. Unless and until otherwise decided by General Meeting, two-fifths of the membership shall be the quorum, subject to the number of members being more than [10] and less than [50].
	b.	In the event of the membership exceeding [50] the quorum shall be [20].
	c.	In the event of the membership being less than [10], the quorum shall be one-half subject to a minimum of [3].

Instituting Change

Clause		Article Text
	d.	An invitation to all members to join an online collaborative decision-making platform before a General Meeting shall be sufficient to satisfy the rules regarding a quorum providing all resolutions on which a vote is required are posted to the online collaborative decision-making platform before the meeting.
	d.	No business shall be transacted at an off-line General Meeting until the meeting has agreed a chairperson. Online General Meetings will not require a chairperson. Whenever a President is in post, the President will chair an off-line General Meeting. If a President is not in post, or the President is not present, the meeting will elect one of the Trustees to chair the meeting. If no Trustee is present, the meeting may elect a chairperson from those present.
19.		The General Meeting can set corporate policy, approve/reject social enterprise plans, and take decisions about acquisition and disposal of property, and partnership arrangements with other organisations.
	a.	A proposal to acquire another organisation may be taken by Ordinary Resolution.
	b.	A proposal to merge with another Association must be put as a Special Resolution.
	c.	A proposal to wind up or dissolve the Association must be put as a Special Resolution.
20		Corporate policy and social enterprise plans are implemented by a Chief Executive Officer or Executive Team appointed by Trustees. The Trustees will stipulate their authority whenever appointed.
	a.	When no Chief Executive Officer or Executive Team is in post, the longest serving Trustee holding a Labour Membership will assume the responsibilities of the Chief Executive Officer until a new Chief Executive Officer or Executive Team can be appointed.
	b.	If the situation in 20(a) arises, and two or more Trustees have the same length of service as a Labour Member, the responsibilities of the Chief Executive Officer shall be shared between them until a new Chief Executive Officer or Executive Team is appointed.
	c.	The Chief Executive Officer or Executive Team is responsible to the General Meeting and Trustees for the organisation and management of the Association and the implementation of the Association's social enterprise plans.

Clause	Article Text
21.	Every Founder, Labour and User Member can attend, speak and propose resolutions at a General Meeting (and in any online General Assembly), can stand (subject to clauses 30 and 31) for election as a Trustee and can cast one vote at General Meetings (except as provided for in clauses 23 and 24).
22.	Any person can act as a proxy for a member at General Meeting. An instrument appointing a proxy must be written in a usual form, or a form approved by the Trustees.
a.	A proxy may act for a maximum of one other member at General Meetings (i.e. can cast a maximum of two votes, including their own).
23.	Decisions at off-line General Meetings are made by passing resolutions with a show of hands, unless a poll is demanded by at least 2 members. In an online General Assembly, decisions are made by approving a member proposal using the collaborative decision-making tools adopted by members.
a.	For Ordinary Resolutions taken by a show of hands (or online vote), Founder, Labour and User members have one vote each irrespective of the class(es) of membership held.
b.	For Ordinary Resolutions where a poll is called, only Labour Members and User Members shall vote. Each member votes once, irrespective of the number of memberships held. Their vote counts toward each member class in which they hold membership. Founder members vote only if they also have a Labour or User membership.
c.	If a poll is requested by at least 2 members, the chairperson must offer each member class a chance to pass a Class Resolution in accordance with the provisions of Clause 25 before proceeding with the poll.
24.	On a show of hands, online vote, or poll, every member who is present in person or by proxy, has one vote.
a.	In the event of a poll, the total number of labour and user votes for and against the resolution will be recalculated using the following formulae: i. [Labour Votes For] / [Labour Votes Cast] * 0.5 ii. [Labour Votes Against] / [Labour Votes Cast] * 0.5 iii. [User Votes For] / [User Votes Cast] * 0.5 iv. [User Votes Against] / [User Votes Cast] * 0.5
b.	The total vote for the resolution is the aggregate of i) and iii)
c.	The total vote against the resolution is the aggregate of ii) and iv)
d.	For the resolution to pass, the aggregate of i) and iii) must be greater than 0.5, otherwise the resolution is not passed.

Instituting Change

Clause	Article Text
	Worked Example – Taking a Poll for an Ordinary Resolution at a General Meeting Labour Votes Cast: 17 Labour Votes For: 5 = 5 / 17 * 50% = 14.7% Labour Votes Against: 12 = 12 / 17 * 50% = 35.3% User Votes Cast: 170 User Votes For: 40 = 40 / 170 * 50% = 11.8% User Votes Against: 130 = 130 / 170 * 50% = 38.2% Total For = 14.7% + 11.8% = 26.5% Total Against = 12% + 24.7% = 73.5% The resolution is defeated.

25.	A Class Resolution **passed by any shareholder class can amend an Ordinary Resolution so that it becomes a Special Resolution** (with the exception of contract terminations described in clause 51).
	  a. A Special Resolution is passed if:
	    i. a majority of votes cast in each member class separately (on a one-member one-vote basis) are in favour of the resolution;
	    ii. at least [75%] of all members cast their vote in favour of the resolution, irrespective of member class, on a one-member one-vote basis.

26.	Unless a poll is demanded, a declaration by the chairperson at the meeting (or announcement in an online forum by the Association) that a resolution has been carried or lost, and an entry to that effect in the book containing the minutes of the proceedings (or equivalent record in an online collaborative decision-making forum) shall be conclusive evidence of the fact without proof of the number or proportions of the votes recorded in favour or against a resolution.
27.	A written resolution signed by all members is valid as if properly passed at a General Meeting.
28.	The proceedings of a meeting are not invalidated by the accidental omission to give notice of the meeting to, or the non-receipt of notice of the meeting by, a person entitled to receive notice.
29.	**Trustees.** The Association shall have a Board of Trustees comprising [three] to [nine] Trustees except in the following circumstances: a. The Association is in receipt of grant or loan funding from a public authority, charitable body or other asset-locked organisation (e.g. a credit union, community benefit society or community interest company), in which case the minimum number of directors shall be three representing at least two member classes, with at least one financial specialist.

Clause		Article Text
	b.	The Association has [50] or more members, in which case the minimum number of Trustees shall be five with at least one representing each shareholder class, with at least one financial specialist.
30.		If the Association has fewer than [50] members, Trustees will be proposed by the Founders or existing Trustees and approved a vote of existing Trustees.
	a.	Trustees may freely negotiate contracts of any value until the Association files its first set of accounts. Thereafter, Trustees may freely negotiate contracts to the value of [25%] of the Association's annual turnover (as reported in the previous year's filed accounts). Contracts in excess of this amount require General Meeting approval.
	b.	A Trustee may be removed at General Meeting by an Ordinary Resolution, or after a vote of no-confidence at a meeting of existing Trustees.
31.		If the Association has [50] or more members, directors and a president will be elected annually as follows.
	a.	Labour Members will elect a maximum of [two] Trustees (one will be subject to re-election by rotation every two-years).
	b.	User Members will elect a maximum of [two] Trustees (one will be subject to re-election by rotation every two-years).
	c.	Founder Members will elect a maximum of [two] Trustees, who may be removed only by the provisions set out in 31(e).
	d.	A maximum of [one] Trustee may be appointed (co-opted) by the other directors for their specialist financial skills.
	e.	A Trustee may be removed from office at any General Meeting by a Class Resolution of a member class that elected him or her, or by Ordinary Resolution.
	f.	A President will be elected from the Trustees on a poll of all members (one vote per member) at the Annual General Meeting. The President has a non-executive role in the running of the Association, and is responsible for overseeing board meetings, maintaining the public image of the Association, and facilitating good communications between Trustees and Association members. The President has a casting vote at board and General Meetings, but is not required to use it.
	g.	In the absence of a President, or if a President is not elected, Founder Members will fulfil this role (as set out in 31(f)).
	h.	A Trustee cannot be removed by other Trustees except at General Meeting (as set out in 31 (e)).

Instituting Change

Clause	Article Text
	i. Trustees may freely negotiate contracts to the value of [12.5%] of the Association's annual turnover (as reported in the previous year's filed accounts). Contracts in excess of this amount require General Meeting approval.
32.	Trustees' meetings may be held between General Meetings by any means defined within the Act, including video and audio conferencing, and through an online collaborative decision-making platform.
	a. All acts done by any meeting of the Trustee Board or by any person acting as a member of the Trustee Board, even if it be afterwards discovered that there was some defect in the appointment of any Trustee or person acting as such, or that they or any of them were disqualified, be as valid as if every such person had been duly appointed and was qualified to be an Trustee.

EXPENSES, BENEFITS AND PAY	
Clause	Article Text
33.	Providers of labour (Trustees, employees, self-employed contractors) shall be paid reasonable expenses wholly incurred in relation to furthering the interests of the Association.
	a. A schedule of acceptable fringe benefits and expenses may be agreed by Ordinary Resolution. Any expenses paid, or fringe benefits provided, outside the scope of an agreed schedule must be itemised in the annual accounts.
	b. Fringe benefits and expenses must be itemised and recorded in such a way that they can be inspected by any member during normal office hours.
34.	**Remuneration** has one component: Basic Wages ("Pay").
	a. Each provider of labour is subject to one or more contracts (employment contract, contract for services or Association membership) which controls the manner in which they are remunerated for their labour. These articles, including subsequent modifications, are part of any contract between the Association and those providing labour (Trustees, shareholders, employees, self-employed contractors). All members of the Association shall be provided with a copy of these rules upon agreement or variation of a contract to supply labour.
	b. Labour may be recognised solely through Association membership. A formal contract of employment will be issued if, in the view of the Trustees, 'employee status' tests used in employment tribunals have been, or are expected to be, satisfied (i.e. a person works regular hours, receives regular

Clause		Article Text
		pay, has agreed holiday entitlements and is subject to regular supervision etc.).
	c.	If the Association issues contracts of employment to members of staff, **the maximum ratio between the hourly rate of the highest and lowest paid member of staff shall be [3:1]**. This ratio can only be amended by a Class Resolution in a meeting of Labour Members. This ratio may **not** be amended by Ordinary Resolution or Special Resolution.
	d.	At the start of each accounting period, if the Association has any employees, an amount equal to (Basic Wages x Current Inflation Rate) will be set aside for increases in Basic Wages. The application of any remuneration system to employees and self-employed contractors is at the discretion of the CEO or Executive Team (unless overridden by the procedure set out in clause 49). If the budget for increases in remuneration is not distributed within an accounting period, any unused part must be distributed to Members' Investor Accounts in equal proportions.
	e.	An increase in the budget set in 34(d) can only be passed by Special Resolution.
	f.	Trustees' do not receive Pay, but will otherwise enjoy the same terms and conditions as other Association members and employees, except where this is in conflict with the Act (where appropriate).
35.	a.	**"Total Revenue"** means sales plus earnings from goods and services provided plus any other income, but excludes proceeds of new issues of securities or loans obtained
	b.	**"Profit"** is equal to Total Revenue less the cost of materials and services, less depreciation, less rents, less interest.
36.		**"Associated Costs"** means the costs directly associated with a given amount of Pay, including employee's and employer's contributions to insurance schemes, superannuation, healthcare plan, childcare, staff club and any other benefits deducted from pay, together with sickness, maternity, paternity or other statutory pay, and Pay-As-You-Earn income tax.
37.		**"Surplus"** is equal to Profit, less Pay including their Associated Costs, less Corporation Tax.
	a.	The first [£10,000] or 30% of Surplus (whichever is greater) will be allocated to Reserves as working capital. This amount will be deducted from Surplus before calculating the credits to pay into members' Investor Accounts (see Clause 15).

Instituting Change

Clause	Article Text
	b. Half of the Surplus transferred to reserves will be held in a **"Social Investment Fund"**, set aside to establish and support organisations to which members have transferred benefits under Clause 11, that enable members to invest in community benefits and public benefits consistent with the objects of the Association.
38.	Additional Capital Expenditure, Extraordinary and Research and Development Costs in excess of [£5,000] not financed by a fundraising campaign must either:
	a. be deducted from Surplus, or
	b. be paid for from Reserves,
	or as determined by Special Resolution or a qualified accountant. Any member may ask a qualified accountant to determine if an item comes under these categories.
39.	**"Labour Share" and "User Share"**. The Labour and User Share of Surplus, distributed as credits to members' Investor Accounts, is calculated by multiplying [Surplus] (if greater than zero) for the relevant period by the [Labour Share Fraction] and [User Share Fraction]. If [Surplus] is less than or equal to zero, no Labour Share or User Share is credited to members' Investor Accounts.
	a. In the event that there are no Labour Members, the Association shall establish or increase a restricted fund to the value of the Labour Share. The Board of Trustees may exercise discretion on how to allocate this restricted fund to projects that improve the well-being of the Association's workforce.
	b. In the event that there are no User Members, the Association shall establish or increase a restricted fund to the value of the User Share. The Board of Trustees may exercise discretion on how to allocate the restricted fund to projects that improve the well-being of the Association's users.
40.	"Labour Share Fraction" and "User Share Fraction"
	a. The Labour Share Fraction is [0.35] and User Share Fraction is [0.35] and may be changed only by Special Resolution.
	b. No Labour or User Shareholder may receive credits to an Investor Account of more than [Surplus] x [Labour Share Fraction].
41.	**"Labour Member Credits" and Restricted Funds for Labour and User Members**
	At the end of an accounting period, the Labour Share is credited *pro rata* to Labour members' Investor Accounts:

Clause		Article Text
	a.	The total Labour Share is distributed pro rata to restricted funds (Labour Member Investor Accounts). If there are no Labour Members, clause 39 applies for the purposes of allocating the fund.
	b.	The total User Share distributed is added to a restricted fund that can be allocated only by User Members. If there are no User Members, clause 39 applies for the purposes of allocating the fund.
	c.	If the Association has Labour Members, the Labour Share shall be managed by them.
	d.	If the Association has User Members, the User Share shall be managed by them.
	e.	The elected representative(s) of Labour Members shall be responsible for convening meetings (either face-to-face or online) of Labour Members to agree social investment projects that are consistent with the objects of the Association. Each Labour Member shall choose individually which project their proportion of the Labour Share shall support.
	f.	The elected representative(s) of User Members shall be responsible for convening meetings of User Members (either face-to-face or online) to agree social investment projects that are consistent with the objects of the Association. User Members shall vote collectively on which projects to support.
42.		No money from the Labour Share or User Share restricted funds may be paid out for the private benefit of individual Labour, User Members or Trustees. The money shall be spent in ways that are consistent with the objects of the Association. For the avoidance of doubt, spending on the welfare needs of Labour and User members shall be deemed *consistent* with the objects of the Association.
43.		No money from the Labour Share or User Share may be paid out for the private benefit of Founder Members.
44.		Investor Account Credits are paid after Labour and User Member Credits.
	a.	The "Investor Share Fraction" is [0.30] and the "Investor Share" is [Surplus] x [Investor Share Fraction]. This may be changed only by special resolution.
	b.	Investor Account credits in any accounting period is the lowest of the following:
		i. the [Investor Share] x (1 − [Capital Gain Fraction]); and
		ii. the balance of the profit and loss account, if greater than zero;
	c.	Otherwise it is zero.

Instituting Change

Clause	Article Text
	d. The Investor Share can be allocated by the Board to projects initiated by members (under 41 (e) and (f) that are consistent with the objects of the Association.
45.	**Shares instead of Credits.** The Trustees may not issue share capital in lieu of Investor Account Credits
46.	Subject to ordinary resolution in a General Meeting, additional sums may be transferred from the profit and loss account to Reserves before Investor Account Credits are calculated.
	ACCOUNTING AND AUDITING
47.	Financial and social accounts will be prepared for the Trustee Board and General Meetings by a person with appropriate bookkeeping and accounting skills / qualifications. They will use accounting conventions agreed by the Trustees, or as required by the Act. Any member or person authorised in writing by a member may inspect the accounting records during normal working hours.
	a. If the Association has fewer than [50] members, the Board may put an ordinary resolution to the General meeting to approve one of the following:
	i. **Either:** the appointment of independent accountants and/or auditors to undertake financial and social audits;
	ii. **Or:** an application for exemption from audit under the relevant accounting regulations;
	b. If the Association has [50] or more members:
	i. The board shall recommend a choice of financial and social auditors for approval in General Meeting.
	ii. The selected financial auditor shall audit the Association's financial accounts prior to their approval in General Meeting for filing with the relevant regulatory authority.
	iii. The selected social auditor shall assist with audit of the internal democracy and decision-making of the Association, the wages, health and safety, skill sharing and educational opportunities of its members and employees, or other matters concerning the overall personal or job satisfaction of members and employees; an assessment of the Association's activities externally, including effects on people, the environment and other organisations.
	iv. An audit committee of up to four people (comprising non-Trustees from at least two member classes) will be elected at each AGM.
	v. The purpose of the audit committee is:

Clause		Article Text
	1.	to assist and check the preparation of financial records presented to General Meetings so that they are accurate, authentic and meet the needs of members;
	2.	to assist and check the preparation of the information needed for a social audit;
	3.	to organise elections in accordance with Clause 31;
	4.	to record, check and authenticate that the procedures in clauses 17 to 27 are being followed when voting takes place in a General Meeting.
48.		Accountants, Auditors and Independent Experts. These must be chosen by ordinary resolution.
	a.	The financial auditor (if appointed) shall be from a Recognised Qualifying Body (RQB).
	b.	All capital invested in the Association by members shall be treated in the accounts as Co-operative Capital.

DISPUTE RESOLUTION AND INTELLECTUAL PROPERTY		
Clause		Article Text
49.		**Labour Contract Revaluations.** In the event of a dispute, the escalation procedure is:
	a.	Valuation by a recruitment agency or recruitment consultant agreeable to all parties.
	b.	Appeal (with resolution) subject to a vote at General Meeting;
	c.	[EXTERNAL MEDIATION SERIVCE]
		In the event that a labour contract revaluation leads to a breach of the ratio between the highest and lowest paid member of staff (as set in clause 34(c)) the revaluation will only be applied if Labour Members pass a Class Resolution adjusting the ratio to permit the new level of pay. Until such time as a Class Resolution is passed, the maximum pay permissible is capped in accordance with the current ratio (e.g. if the ratio is 3:1, the maximum pay is 3x the lowest paid).
50.		**Relationship Disputes.** In the event of a dispute between two or more members, the escalation procedure is:
	a.	Mediation by the President, or Trustee, a management consultant, trade union official, Co-operative Body official, Social Enterprise Europe Director, FairShares Association Founder, or other third-party agreeable to all parties;
	b.	Appeal (with resolution) subject to a vote at General Meeting;
	c.	[EXTERNAL MEDIATION SERVICE]

Instituting Change

Clause	Article Text
51.	Except in the case of resignation or voluntary termination by both parties, a member's employment, supplier contract (or Association membership) may be terminated only after an Ordinary Resolution proposing the termination of the contract has been passed in General Meeting.
	a. Termination is subject to the satisfaction of all lawful terms contained in the member's employment and/or trading contract(s). A resolution to terminate an employment or supplier contract, or Association membership, cannot be modified by Class Resolution to become a Special Resolution (clause 25 does not apply).
52.	The Association may pay for Trustees' and officers' indemnity insurance against liabilities related to Association business, excluding negligence and/or fraud.
53.	**Intellectual Property (IP).** The Association shall record which members have created and contributed intellectual property (IP) to further Association objects, and ensure that ownership of all IP remains vested in its creator(s). For the avoidance of doubt, the Association shall not own IP created by members before, during or after their period of membership unless ownership is freely and voluntarily transferred by those members to the Association.
	a. All IP created by members while working for the Association will be vested in them individually and/or collectively.
	b. As a condition of membership and/or employment, all IP created by members during their work for the Association shall be licensed to the Association under a Creative Commons Licence for both non-commercial and commercial trading, with permission to adapt, share and re-use the IP in product and service development. Any product or service offered will use the same Creative Commons licence unless a variation of this is negotiated with the creator(s) of the IP.
	i. Where a member creates (or members create) IP for the Association during their period of membership, the Association shall have an exclusive right to use and commercialise the IP while they remain a member. If the member leaves the Association, upon termination of their membership, the Association shall retain a non-exclusive right to continue using and adapting their IP in both non-commercial and commercial ventures.
	ii. Members who leave the Association retain a non-exclusive right to use IP they created for the Association in both non-commercial and commercial ventures.

Clause		Article Text
	c.	IP transferred to the Association by members, and IP bought by the Association from third parties, shall be owned collectively by all members and made freely available to them for non-commercial use and private study.
	d.	The Association shall use its best endeavours to manage IP as if it were an 'intellectual commons' for the benefit of Association members.

		DISSOLUTION
54.		Upon dissolution, a qualified accountant or auditor will calculate the value of **"residual assets"** ([Investor Accounts] + [accumulated profit and loss account] + [assets – liabilities]). After satisfaction of all creditors, **residual assets** will be distributed as a **"community dividend"** to other Associations, Co-operatives and FairShares or Community Interest Companies that share the objects of the Association:
	a.	The Association may specify which organisations the **community dividend** will be distributed to. Unless otherwise agreed in writing, it will be divided equally between the following bodies:

Organisation Name:
FairShares / CIC No:
or Charity / Foundation / Association No:
or Association Registration Number:

Organisation Name:
FairShares / CIC No:
or Charity / Foundation / Association No:
or Cooperative Registration Number:

Organisation Name:
FairShares / CIC No:
or Charity / Foundation / Association No:
or Association Registration Number:

	b.	In finalising the dissolution of the Association, and subject to the requirements of Insolvency Law, debts and payments to creditors and shareholders will be satisfied in the following order:
		i. Outstanding debts to **employees, workers and contractors** (e.g. wages/fees)
		ii. Outstanding debts to other **priority creditors** (e.g. VAT and taxes)

Instituting Change

   iii. Outstanding debts to **suppliers** (e.g. unpaid supplier invoices)

   iv. Outstanding debts to **other creditors** (e.g. loan balances)

   v. Payment of the community dividend

 c. In the event of a failure to agree within 6 months of dissolution which association(s), cooperatives(s) and companies should receive the community dividend, or in the event that the organisations in Clause 54(a) have all closed, the [community dividend] will be donated to the FairShares Association Ltd to be reinvested in other FairShares associations, cooperatives and companies.

Appendix A – Values and Principles

Brand guidelines

Version 2.1, 1st July 2015.

Introduction

The *FairShares Model* is a brand and concept advanced by the FairShares Association to assist the creation of FairShares enterprises. At the heart of the brand is the definition of social enterprise established by Social Enterprise Europe Ltd in 2012 based on:

1. Specifying social purpose(s) and evaluating the social, environmental and economic impact(s) of trading;
2. Conducting ethical reviews of product/service offers and production/consumption processes;
3. Promoting socialised and democratic ownership, governance and management by primary stakeholders.

Brand principles

The brand can be used by associations, cooperatives, companies, consultancies and educators to communicate their commitment to:

1. wealth and power sharing amongst primary stakeholders;
2. ethically sourced goods and services;
3. sustainable production and consumption practices;
4. the pursuit of social purpose(s) and social impact(s);
5. socialised (democratic) models of ownership, governance and management.

Levels of alignment

1. **Level 1** – an enterprise actively disseminates the FairShares Model, but there is little evidence that the brand principles are applied to itself.
2. **Level 2** – an enterprise actively supports use of the FairShares Model and implements the brand principles using proprietary / alternative design principles
3. **Level 3** – an enterprise actively supports use of the FairShares Model and puts them into practice by adopting (and adapting) FairShares IP and/or model constitution.

In the *FairShares Model*, **primary** stakeholders are regarded as:

1. Producers and employees (i.e. those who do the work of the organisation)
2. Consumer and service users (i.e. those who depend on its products and services).

*If a FairShares Enterprise does not integrate producers, employees, consumers or users into ownership, governance and management, it is not conforming to the FairShares brand guidelines. Founder members and investors are regarded as **secondary stakeholders** if they are not directly engaged in the production of, or usage of, the goods and services that the enterprise creates.*

On Ownership, Governance and Management, a Level 2 / 3 FairShares association / cooperative / cooperative society / consultancy or educator will:

1. recognise founder members and enfranchise them through **Founder Shares / Founder Membership**;
2. recognise providers of labour and enfranchise them through **Labour Shares / Labour Membership;**
3. recognise users/customers and enfranchise them through **User Shares / User Membership;**
4. recognise creators and providers of financial capital by enfranchising them through **Investor Shares** or contracts to fund projects.

On Intellectual Property (IP), a Level 3 FairShares Enterprise will:

1. give individual and group recognition to members who create IP;
2. agree Creative Commons licences for the use of members' IP;
3. prevent the transfer of IP from members to an enterprise unless the transfer is initiated by the IP creator(s);
4. manage members' IP as an Intellectual Commons on behalf of all members.

Brand variants

All FairShares Enterprises issue Founder Shares / Membership and manage an Intellectual Commons on behalf of members:

1. A Level 2/3 FairShares *solidarity enterprise* also issues Labour, User and Investor Shares (company law);
2. A Level 2/3 FairShares *solidarity cooperative* also issues Labour, User and Investor Shares (cooperative law);
3. A Level 2/3 FairShares *solidarity association* also admits User and Labour Members (association / charity law);
4. A Level 2/3 FairShares *employee-owned company* also issues Labour and Investor Shares (company law);
5. A Level 2/3 FairShares *worker cooperative* also issues Labour and Investor Shares (cooperative law);
6. A Level 2/3 FairShares *labour association* also admits Labour Members (association / charity law);
7. A FairShares Level 2/3 *user-owned company* also issues User and Investor Shares (company law);
8. A Level 2/3 FairShares *user cooperative* also issues User and Investor Shares (cooperative law);
9. A Level 2/3 FairShares *user association* also admits User Members (association / charity law).

The FairShares Model is licensed to the FairShares Association by Rory Ridley-Duff and Cliff Southcombe using a Creative Commons licence:

Values and Principles

© Rory Ridley-Duff, Cliff Southcombe and
FairShares Association Ltd, 2015
Creative Commons 4.0: Attribution, Share Alike.

All variants and adaptations of the *FairShares Model* must acknowledge the copyright holders in the above format, and new adaptations must carry the same Creative Commons licence.

Brand identity

Logos for printed and electronic use are available to supporters and members in PNG and SVG format to identify support for the *FairShares Model*.

Brand values and social auditing

To advance the brand, a FairShares enterprise should be able to offer persuasive answers to the following questions:

1. What is the *purpose* of your enterprise?
2. How are the social, environmental and economic impacts of your trading assessed?
3. What *values and principles* guide the choice of goods and services that you offer?
4. What *values and principles* guide the production and (re)sale of those goods and services?
5. Who are the enterprise's *primary stakeholders*?
6. How do the ownership, governance and management systems ensure an *equitable distribution of wealth and power* amongst primary stakeholders?

Appendix B - Resources

The Dragons' Apprentice: a social enterprise novel

Fast forward to 2032. In a cooperative world full of social enterprises, the BBC hires a new quartet of Dragons...

Warren is an entrepreneur who has successfully amassed billions. Unfortunately, since receiving an ASBO for anti-social investing, he has been banned from starting any new ventures. Then he receives a call from Sharon - an ambitious producer at the BBC – to ask if he would like to put his unemployed capital back to work on a new game show. Should he accept?

Dr Rory Ridley-Duff is Reader in Cooperative and Social Enterprise at Sheffield Business School, a director of Social Enterprise Europe Ltd, and is a co-founder of the FairShares Association. He is an editorial board member of the Social Enterprise Journal and Chair of the Principles of Responsible Management Group at Sheffield Business School. His book, *Understanding Social Enterprise: Theory and Practice* (co-authored with Mike Bull) is used by educators on four continents.

His other books include:
- **Silent Revolution**: creating and managing social enterprises;
- **Friends or Lovers;**
- **Emotion, Seduction and Intimacy**: alternative perspectives on human behaviour;
- **Understanding Social Enterprise**: theory and practice.

~~mcontent.com/pod-product-compliance
,ce LLC
ɟ PA
ɔ6170526
ɜ00001B/269